THE CHANGING OF THE GODS

THE CHANGING OF THE GODS

FRANK E. MANUEL

PUBLISHED FOR BROWN UNIVERSITY PRESS

 BY UNIVERSITY PRESS OF NEW ENGLAND

HANOVER AND LONDON, 1983

UNIVERSITY PRESS OF NEW ENGLAND

BRANDEIS UNIVERSITY
BROWN UNIVERSITY
CLARK UNIVERSITY
DARTMOUTH COLLEGE
UNIVERSITY OF NEW HAMPSHIRE
UNIVERSITY OF RHODE ISLAND
TUFTS UNIVERSITY
UNIVERSITY OF VERMONT

Materials from previously published work by the author have been corrected, revised, or expanded for use in the present collection. Grateful acknowledgment is made for permission to reprint from the following:

"The Philosophes and the Psychology of Everyday Religion," in *Religion in the 18th Century,* ed. R. E. Morton and J. D. Browning (New York: Garland Publishing, 1979), pp. 59–75 (© 1979 McMaster University Association for 18th-Century Studies).

"Edward Gibbon: Historien-Philosophe," *Daedalus,* Summer 1976, pp. 231–245.

"Israel and the Enlightenment," *Daedalus,* Winter 1982, pp. 33–52.

Johann Gottfried von Herder, *Reflections on the Philosophy of the History of Mankind,* Editor's Introduction (Chicago: University of Chicago Press, 1968), pp. ix–xxv (© 1968 by The University of Chicago).

LIBRARY OF CONGRESS CATALOGING IN PUBLICATION DATA

Manuel, Frank Edward.
   The changing of the gods.

   Includes bibliographical references and index.
   Contents: Three scientists in search of God—Deists on true and false gods—A psychology of everyday religion—[etc.]
   1. Religion—Philosophy—Addresses, essays, lectures.
2. Enlightenment—Addresses, essays, lectures.   I. Title.
BL51.M334   1983   200'.9'032   82-40475
ISBN 0-87451-254-9

CONTENTS

INTRODUCTION

I n virtually every European language there is a label for the sweeping movement of thought that began sometime in the seventeenth century and ended with the decade of the French Revolution. In French it was *les lumières,* usually joined with the time-period as *Siècle des lumières;* in German, *Aufklärung;* in English, Enlightenment; in Italian, *illuminismo,* in Spanish, *ilustración.* The variations on "light" are probably related to religious experience, and there may be a covert critical intent behind the imagery: the secular worldly enlightenment is authentic, unlike the specious enlightenment of the mystics, who tried to preempt the metaphor of light to convey their esoteric communion with the divine. The nomenclature became confusing when a sect of eighteenth-century German religious enthusiasts proclaimed themselves *illuminati* in the old, not the new sense, and supporters of the Great Awakening, the religious revival in the Connecticut Valley of New England, were identified as the "new lights," in contradistinction to the "old lights," whose Calvinist religion had turned rationalist. The phrase *despotisme éclairé,* enlightened despotism, was an implicit condemnation of *despotisme oriental* (usually Turkish), which had a pejorative connotation in the eighteenth century.

The enlightenments of the various national societies differed from one another, even though there was a recognition among adherents that the movement of ideas was European, or, as they described it with the characteristic Europocentrism of the time, "cosmopolitan." But if enlightenment was perceived as a cosmopolitan historical phenomenon, there was an awareness that it had an uneven development in various parts of the world. Toward the end of the century men like Turgot and Condorcet had in their mind's eye a geography of enlightenment that was a study in chiaroscuro: the globe could be mapped with black areas, Africa and Asia, and portions on both sides of the Atlantic that were totally illuminated. Light was constantly being diffused from great urban centers (the headquarters were Paris and London), and the penetration of the darkest corners of the earth by the end of the century was considered inevitable.

The best summations of enlightenment came, as might be expected, at the end of the period and not at the beginning. For French society the canonical text was Condorcet's *Esquisse d'un tableau historique des progrès de l'esprit humain (Sketch of a Historical Picture of the Progressions of the Human Mind)*, 1795, a world history of enlightenment in nine stages leading up to the present and then projected into a future tenth stage. Kant's essay of 1784, *Beantwortung der Frage: Was ist Aufklärung* ("An Answer to the Query: What is Enlightenment"), also arrived post festum, after the enlightenment had passed its peak. His remains the classical definition aimed primarily against the blind acceptance of religious authority. "Enlightenment is the liberation of man from his self-caused state of minority. Minority is the incapacity of using one's understanding without the direction of another. The state of minority is self-caused when its source lies not in lack of understanding, but in lack of determination and courage to use it without the assistance of another. *Sapere aude.* Dare to use your own understanding! is then the motto of Enlightenment."

Englishmen and Germans began to react against the values of the Enlightenment before the French Revolution and the blood of the Terror, which heightened their antagonism; but the Revolution provided a convenient cutoff point, even though many of the challenges to the dominant ideas of the age had been issued earlier. In many ways the age of the Enlightenment was given shape and form for the nineteenth century by its enemies. Hamann and Herder in East Prussia, Samuel Johnson, Burke, and Blake in

England, rebelled against what they considered the constrictions of the Enlightenment. They wrested away from it the imagery of illumination and restored it to traditionalist religious experience. Blake made antiheroes of Locke and Newton, the gods of eighteenth-century thought, and sneered at the tirades of Voltaire and Rousseau as futile:

> Mock on, Mock on Voltaire, Rousseau:
> Mock on, Mock on: 'tis all in vain!
> You throw the sand against the wind,
> And the wind blows it back again.

A heterogeneous group of philosophical thinkers was cast into a net of guilt by association and held responsible for the excesses of the Revolution. Driven to seek a cause for the breakdown of the political structure of the largest national society in Europe, Burke discovered the philosophical cabal, a plot to destroy the religious foundations of civilized society; the poet Béranger later jested, "C'est la faute à Voltaire, c'est la faute à Rousseau."

Thinkers of the nineteenth century defined themselves by negating the thought of the eighteenth, even as many eighteenth-century writers achieved their own identity by raising specters of an earlier epoch, conjuring up the cruelties of the bigoted Middle Ages. Eighteenth-century thinkers made a stereotype of the period from the fall of Rome to the renaissance of arts and letters; the early nineteenth century reduced the Enlightenment to a set of clichés. In both cases complexities were overlooked and nuances of thought brushed aside.

These seven essays are concerned with one aspect of the Enlightenment, religious belief and disbelief. The time may have passed for delivery in the grand manner of a new Leviathan on Enlightenment thought as a whole. Yet the fish I lay before you are not a random catch. Religion in the Enlightenment has occupied me for many years, ever since I first tried to capture the mind and sensibility of that age by studying its theories of ancient pagan myth as projections of inner feeling. In some ways the present book is an extension of *The Eighteenth Century Confronts the Gods*

(1959), but there has been a shift in the subject matter: In the older work paganism was at the epicenter, here the gods of Christianity and Judaism are directly engaged.

The first essay, "Three Scientists in Search of God," looks at the relations of science and religion through the eyes of three men of genius with more than formal attachment to the religions into which they were born and baptized—Kepler the Lutheran, Galileo the Catholic, and Newton the Anglican. I have tried to highlight their individual efforts to conciliate the Book of Nature and the Book of Scriptures as two sources of one divine truth. Since I have already written on Newton's chronological and mythological theories, his religion, and his character, that part of the essay devoted to Newton is an exercise in brevity. Kepler and Galileo, learned exegetes of the Bible in their own right, are reminders of the dangers threatening scientists who invaded the sacristy in the early part of the seventeenth century. In "Deists on True and False Gods," an English heresy nurtured in the bosom of the Anglican Church is conceived as a new view of Christianity, the rational religion of the Enlightenment that transforms the philosopher-pagans of the ancient world into ideal figures worthy of emulation and distinguishes them from the superstitious masses. "A Psychology of Everyday Religion" addresses itself to the question of how the radical English and French thinkers translated into literary psychological language the practices of popular religious belief and related them to their theories of human nature. The traditional philosophical proofs of the existence of God and their refutation were bypassed, as these men strove to offer some psychological explanation for what they regarded as manifestly absurd human behavior. I treat the new religion of Rousseau and the German glorification of the ordinary man's emotional piety as part of a revolutionary countermovement.

"A Godless History" is a commentary on the underlying principles of Gibbon's classical history of the Roman Empire, which ignored the intervention of God in human affairs except for satirical anticlerical asides. The secular mechanism that replaced Providence is analyzed in the light of the Humean moral values that

Gibbon favored and the theatrical mainsprings of action that he sought to reveal. "Israel in the Christian Enlightenment" explores the prickly problem of the continued existence of Judaism in a European culture which no longer held firmly to inherited justifications for the survival of a religion that denied Christ. The subject is not the hackneyed issue of Jewish toleration and emancipation in the Enlightenment, but Christian society's reappraisal, on the theological and intellectual level, of the ancient God of the Jews. In "Theodicy of a Pietist" the thought of Herder the Lutheran pastor is presented as a theodicy of Leibnizian dimensions and inspiration. Herder's providential philosophy of history, fundamentally at odds with the Augustinian war of the men of the two cities, was an attempt to rescue religion from the attacks of the critical *philosophes*. It ended up as a theodicy, a justification of God's way in the world. "The Triadic Metaphor" dwells on the persistence of the Christian formula in eighteenth-century utopias that would usher in a heaven on earth. The manner in which age-old Christian religious patterns were assimilated into secular philosophies is illustrated from the writings of a heterogeneous company of European thinkers, many of whom were ordained priests and ministers of church establishments.

The voyages of discovery that began in the late fifteenth century initiated a steady flow of reports from explorers, conquerors, missionaries, and independent travelers that in passing speculated about the religion of savages and the meaning of ritual observances in the high civilizations encountered in Mexico, Peru, Persia, and China. Europeans were quick to recognize conformities between the practices of the contemporary pagans and the pagans of ancient Greece and Rome. Almost simultaneously, another body of literature was accumulating on religion itself—Christian, Jewish, and pagan—as a human experience. The seventeenth-century European who ventured to write about religion as rooted in human nature or as a historical event, rather than as a revelation from God, was an apostate commenting on his own creed or the member of a Christian denomination denouncing false doctrines and disputing with rivals. The true believer of one Christian sect might freely deploy the instrumentalities of logic and historical criticism in demolishing the dogmas of another. The writer assumed the role of an outsider, and the religion he observed was turned into an object that was no longer privileged and sacred. When Spinoza separated himself off from the synagogue and wrote the first revolutionary account of the Bible as a historical document in the *Tractatus Theologico-Politicus (Theologico-Political Treatise)*, 1670, he categorized types of prophecy as if he were a scientist arranging specimens for a natural history. Henry More's dissection of religious enthusiasm, a rationalist Anglican attack on papal and dissenter fanaticism, was a clinical analysis of a deadly error that others later extended to embrace all religion.

In both their belief and their disbelief, men of the Enlightenment were profoundly agitated by religion as an expression of human nature. While conventional doctrinal disputations continued to pour forth from rival sectarians, the *philosophes* posed questions about the essence of religion in a new language. In mid-eighteenth-century France, a brazen group of writers, the Holbachians, became preoccupied with religion as a disease, and they charted its course in order to eradicate it or at least render it harmless. While their works, usually published in Holland and smuggled into France, treated religious questions with wild indiscretion, most *philosophes* exercised a measure of caution. Voltaire, Montesquieu, Hume, Gibbon, and Diderot as editor of the *Encyclopédie* were always conscious of the power of the official religious establishments and they took cover behind Aesopian language. But despite the evasiveness of some and the provocative blatancy of others, the *philosophes* were able to leave behind a substantial number of treatises in which they interpreted religion as they would any other natural phenomenon. The theories were not always consonant one with another, but the writings constitute a corpus of thought on the origins of religion and its psychological and sociological consequences for mankind. Without knowing it, the *philosophes* founded a science of religion.

For a brief period during the French Revolution, under the Directorate, it was possible for members of the Institut de France to conduct inquiries into religious behavior without official ecclesiastical oversight, but this was a passing moment, and the analysts of religion in the first half of the nineteenth century were not able to maintain their complete independence. It was left to aliens like Feuerbach and Marx, who never held university posts, to advance daring new hypotheses about the etiology of religion. The next venturesome anatomy of religion comparable in scope to that of the *philosophes* was not undertaken until the end of the nineteenth century, when religion became an academic topic in the secular university. Soon philosophers like Bergson and William James and sociologists like Durkheim and Weber tackled the subject in new ways. Nietzsche and Freud scandalized believers with their heterodox opinions, and the flowering of modern sciences of anthropology and mythology revived questions on the nature of religion that had once been resolved to their own satisfaction by the *philosophes*.

Self-conscious exploration of religious behavior has been a perennial theme of Western culture. In many respects the eighteenth-century interpretations were elaborations, made forceful with contemporary empirical data, of insights that had already found embryonic expression in the writings of the ancient Greeks and Romans and the Church Fathers. Similarly, Enlightenment reflections were incorporated by nineteenth- and twentieth-century commentators on religious experience. The chain of Western absorption with understanding in rational terms man's religious propensity—the phrase is William James's—is virtually unbroken, and in its variety and intricacy has no equivalent among the Chinese, the Hindus, or any other major culture. The manner of these seven soundings in the religion of the age is discursive. My intention is to describe and reflect, argue as little as possible, and illustrate the richness of Enlightenment thought on the nature of religion without forcing its many brilliant insights into a set of common propositions.

1 THREE SCIENTISTS
IN SEARCH OF GOD

E UROPE in the seventeenth century was a traditional society in turmoil: It was shaken by social and political crises, as well as fratricidal warfare among the dynasts in which religious loyalties played a significant, though not a determining, role. In all states—Catholic, Lutheran, Calvinist, or Anglican—intellectual and spiritual institutions were by their very nature conservative, and ecclesiastical authorities were jealous of their prerogatives. Doubtless there were men in religious establishments who were prepared to welcome the new science in some measure so long as its practitioners, an amorphous assemblage without a formal collective name until the nineteenth century, introduced it slowly, without fanfare, in driblets, practically unnoticed. The conduct of William Harvey was a model of discretion. He quietly presented his theory on the circulation of the blood within a traditional Aristotelian framework, and nobody was dismayed. Even the greatest of innovators, Isaac Newton, at times maintained rather modestly that he had merely rediscovered what ancient philosophers, under the mask of myth-makers, had once taught. But scientific activity in a thousand shapes—alchemical, Paracelsian, academic, experimental—was becoming too conspicuous to be simply ignored, assimilated, or silently accommodated by the old spiritual order without creating a ripple.

The practice of science as a virtuous pursuit in Christian, aristocratic, seventeenth-century Europe should not be taken for granted. It had to overcome the inveterate prejudices of different segments of the population, and not only the obduracy of the ecclesiastical establishments. One group of the religious looked upon the absorption with secondary causes as a deflection from contemplation of the divine Primary Cause and hence suspect, if not heretical, especially when propositions like the Copernican hypothesis seemed to contradict the literal sense of the Bible. Aristocrats who had an Aristotelian contempt for manual labor and a certain fastidiousness in personal habit were offended by the very idea of a man of quality dirtying his bare hands with offal and black coals and animal carcasses. The mass of the people, not free from the image of the scientist as a sorcerer or one possessed by the devil, were frightened by clandestine experiments said to bestow dark powers upon the natural philosopher. And some literary wits, beginning to be jealous of the honors heaped upon men who toyed with rulers and triangles and circles rather than lofty poesy, soon found an easy mark for ridicule in the portrait of the obsessed scientist.

I

The sheer accumulation and increasing weight of the new science made a clash with its detractors inevitable. When there is a confrontation in which rival corps such as scientists and ecclesiastics do not seek to annihilate each other completely (with the possible exception of Giordano Bruno, I recognize no pretenders to the total destruction of the existing spiritual order, and even his purposes are too wild, changeable, and ambivalent to be readily categorized), they try to invent myths or metaphors that delimit jurisdictions, prevent frictions and encroachments, and ensure mutual forbearance, if not interdependence. An intellectual metaphor adopted by an age is often a passionate attempt to forge at least the appearance of a solution to an almost insoluble problem. Since the subject was critical at a vital turning point in European culture, the verbal and imaginative structures it created, or borrowed from previous ages and adapted, are worthy of examination in their own right. Baldly stated two major conceptions evolved during the course of the seventeenth century about the possible relations of science and religion in European society. One can be subsumed under the broadly used metaphor of the two books, the Book of Nature and the Book of Scriptures, both considered equal sources of Christian knowledge, both leading to truth but remaining separate, with distinct languages, modes of expression, institutional arrangements, and areas of specialization. The other myth, far more fanciful in character, was the ideal of pansophia, a new Christian synthesis of organic truth that would replace the relatively stable body of beliefs Europe had supposedly entertained around the year 1500, prior to the great religious schisms and the serious attacks on the inherited conceptual framework of Ptolemy, Aristotle, and Galen—to use an abbreviation for the science that had become acceptable to the churches of Europe. Among many theorists pansophia entailed a virtual integration of the two spiritual corps, the scientists and the ministers of religion, into a single body.

Two such conceptions immediately raise as many questions as they answer, both because they are antagonistic to each other and because they betray palpable internal difficulties. Understanding what transpired in the course of the century involves a bookish study of rational arguments, of warranties from sacred texts, and of emotive longings expressed in philosophical dialogues and private letters. In addition to the metaphor of the two books and pansophia, there was of course a third attitude on the relations of science and religion, that of the mathematician Pascal turned Jansenist, the outright denial of any intrinsic worth to the works of science in a deepened religious consciousness; but analysis of his thought and its implications is beyond the bounds of our subject.

The people who did most of the writing on the relations of science and religion in the seventeenth century can be roughly divided into three types. First, those who were the trumpeters of the new science, men who were not themselves virtuosi or investiganti, but who either heralded the new creators or drafted programs for them. By definition they were apologists and defenders who tried to work out a favorable relationship with religion for the new philosophy. Bacon in England and Campanella in Italy and Andreae in Germany are exemplary figures of this character, writing at about the same time. Comenius repeats the attempt in the next generation. Then there were the major scientists themselves, especially Kepler, Galileo, and Newton, who in moments of crisis when they were being attacked or an attack from some quarter was imminent, or for a variety of personal reasons, recorded their own religious ideas, or wrote about the relations of the two books, or dreamed of the future of European Christian man in a new Christian republic that would recognize the autonomy of science. Finally, there were the philosophers—Descartes and Spinoza, Locke and Leibniz—who on a more abstract level than the trumpeters or the scientists themselves, sought to draw the implications of what was going on. This tripartite division among the protagonists does not lock any individual into a single role, for some seventeenth-century men of genius appeared in all three parts at one time or another in their lives and works.

The enemies of science, men ensconced in positions of spiritual power, were a vital part of the conflict. But they do not yield as rich a harvest of thought as those engaged in some way with advancing the new philosophy. The outlook of the traditionalists emerges in disputation with the defenders of science. The churchmen were not always devils; some were fools, some showed their teeth, and a few were wise men with a philosophical predilection for spiritual compromise with the new forces. The last group found the metaphor of the two books particularly useful, as did many working scientists.

II

Back in the sixteenth century, Calvin's teachings set a precedent for the separation of the two books that perhaps made toleration of the new scientific philosophy somewhat easier among those Christian sects that were either Calvinist or under Calvinist influence in their theology. In this sphere the doctrinal distinction between Puritanism and Anglicanism is not fundamental, though it *is* in their politics and church organization. The impossible task of defining a Puritan is avoided and one is freed from the intellectual shackles of a causal relationship between Puritanism and science. In the light of Calvin's doctrinal attitude there may be some point to the accusations made by members of the Lutheran consistory that Kepler, baptized a Lutheran, was flirting with Calvinism.

Calvin's most important declaration on science occurs in his *Commentaries on the First Book of Moses, called Genesis,* where, after attacking the Catholic allegorical interpretations of Genesis, he supported a Talmudic view handed down by the dominant group of medieval Jewish commentators and integrated into many schools of Christian exegesis: The Bible speaks in the language of everyman. About the Mosaic account of the Creation Calvin wrote:

[I]t is not here philosophically discussed, how great the sun is in the heaven, and how great, or how little, is the moon; but how much light comes to us from them. For Moses here addresses himself to our senses, that the knowledge of the gifts of God which we enjoy may not glide away. . . . By this method . . . the dishonesty of those men is sufficiently rebuked, who censure Moses for not speaking with greater exactness. For as it became a theologian, he had respect to *us* rather than to the stars. . . . Moses wrote in a popular style things which, without instruction, all ordinary persons, endued with common sense, are able to understand; but astronomers investigate with great labour whatever the sagacity of the human mind can comprehend. Nevertheless, this study is not to be reprobated, nor this science to be condemned, because some frantic persons are wont boldly to reject whatever is unknown to them. For astronomy is not only pleasant, but also very useful to be known: it cannot be denied that this art unfolds the admirable wisdom of God. Wherefore, as ingenious men are to be honoured who have expended useful labour on this subject, so they who have leisure and capacity ought not to neglect this kind of exercise. Nor did Moses truly wish to withdraw us from this pursuit in omitting such things as are peculiar to the art; but because he was ordained a teacher as well of the unlearned and rude as of the learned, he could not otherwise fulfil his office than by descending to this grosser method of instruction.[1]

Lambert Daneau, in a work translated into English as *The Wonderfull Woorkmanship of the World,* continued to respect Mosaic science in the tradition of Calvin.

Verily, I confesse, that these matters concerning Naturall Philosophie, are not gloriously and in a filed style set foorth by *Moses* although hee were the beste learned man that ever lyved, but rather in a bare and simple kinde of writinge, striped out of all ornament, as it were out of apparrell, wherby that which hee writeth may the more easily bee understood. But, as it is to bee graunted that hee spake simply, so can it not bee prooved that hee spake or wrote lyingly, falsely, and ignorantly of those thinges. It is one thing therfore, to acknowledg that *Moses* stile is bare and simple, which kinde of utteraunce is meet for the truth: and another thing to say that hee is a false man and a lyar: which no man can affirme, but whoso is of a corrupt conscience. Wherfore simply, but truely: barely, but rightly: commonly, but purely, doth hee deliver unto us those thinges which hee writeth, concerning the worlde, of the principall partes thereof, of the causes and effectes of thinges, to bee beleeved, holden, and taughte among menne. Verily, I confesse, that *Moses* applyed himselfe to ye capacitie of our senses.[2]

Daneau had a historical explanation, plausible in its day, for Moses' knowledge of astronomy. Since science was highly prized in Egypt, Moses had learned it from the priests there. In their turn, Daneau assures us, quoting Diogenes Laertius, Plato and Pythagoras acquired their astronomical knowledge from the Syrians, and who are the Syrians but the Jews? One Moschus the Phoenician was their teacher, and Moschus was no other than Moses, an etymological identification that persisted in the Protestant world at least as late as Isaac Newton. And if these arguments were not sufficient to convince men of Moses' pre-eminence in science—which at the same time made the new science respectable—Daneau asked rhetorically:

Shal we say then, against ye assured faith of ye scripture that any one of the cheifest Philosophers, to wit, *Plato* or *Aristotle,* whiche were heathen men, were called by GOD to counsell when hee went to framinge and creatinge of the worlde, that they shoulde knowe more than *Moses* the servaunt of GOD, whom God himselfe taught, and shewed unto him such things as hee should commit to writinge to the behoofe of Posteritie, and especially for the instruction of his moste deerely beeloved Church?[3]

As the seventeenth century advanced, this delineation of Moses as at once the most learned of scientists and a popularizer of science could direct men along two separate paths, though they might crisscross from time to time. One was emphasis on the popular language of Moses. The other led to the creation of a branch of knowledge that was later termed *Physica Sacra* and had an extraordinary development in Newton's circle: with exegetical skill the major elements of the new physical system of the world were found concealed in Genesis.

As the studies of the great Christian Hebraists—men like Selden, Lightfoot, Pocock, and John Spencer in England, Vossius father and son and Reeland on the Continent—multiplied in the course of the century, there was a growing tendency to draw what was considered to be a realistic portrait of the condition of the Israelites at the time Moses was addressing them in Sinai about the Creation. The idea gained currency, especially in the English and Dutch worlds, where biblical scholarship flourished, that the various books of the Bible were written in different periods and under diverse circumstances, and the conviction took root that their sundry authors had expressed themselves in accordance with the particular spirit of the times in which they lived. This absolved scientists from the necessity of accepting a literal interpretation of Scriptures as absolutely true natural philosophy, or of resorting to allegory to explain away what their reason could not tolerate. Making allowance for the *ingenium* of the age was an important innovation, though only a few men dared to go the way of Spinoza in the *Tractatus Theologico-Politicus* and construe the Mosaic document in all its parts as exclusively and solely a political-moral treatise addressed to one historical people at a given moment and applicable only to their moral training.

Instead of attempting to encompass the whole vast field of science and religion, I have singled out three intellectual giants of the age—Kepler in Germany, Galileo in Italy, and Newton in England—in order to examine the terms of the relationship between the two books by which they lived. Their views serve as a prolegomenon to the average literate European's wrestling with many questions of belief and disbelief raised by the new science. Their experiences illustrate the inherent difficulties of accepting

a separation between the realms of science and of religion in a society that remains Christian, especially when the scientists themselves believe that they are no mean knowers of scriptural truth.

III

Though on first impression Kepler and Galileo would seem to
have placed the Book of Nature and the Book of Scriptures on a
fairly equal footing, the more one reads their works and letters,
the more evident it becomes that their new science was not content
with seeking mere equality of status. They broadly hinted that
their book, the Book of Nature, was superior and brought men
even closer to the Creator than could Scriptures. At times the scientists still sound apologetic in tone. Kepler asks equality for the
finger of God with the word of God; Galileo glorifies the manifestations of the hand of God; Newton in his letters to Bentley is
pleased that the *Principia* will help men recognize the impress of
the arm of God (I am unable to account for this creeping progression of anthropomorphisms). And yet the mounting *hubris* of the
scientists soon becomes apparent.

In the "Introduction" to the *Nova Astronomia,* Kepler begs his
reader when he returns from the Temple of Religion to enter the
School of Astronomy, where he will imbibe the real wisdom and
greatness of the Creator as disclosed by Kepler and learn the real
explication of the world's frame. If he comprehends Kepler's dis-
quisition on the true causes of things and the way to correct errors
of sight, the reader will not only extol the bounty of God for the
establishment of the world and the preservation of living creatures
of all kinds, about which he can learn from the Bible and sense
experience, but he will also become informed about the earth's
motion, a phenomenon so strange and marvelous he will have to
acknowledge that here too the wisdom of the Creator may be discerned. So far so good. Then Kepler suddenly launches into a
"consilium pro idiotis," advice to the ignorant, and berates those
who are so stupid as not to comprehend the science of astronomy
or so boorish as to think it an offense to piety to adhere to Coper-
nicus. "Let them go home and manure their fields" and not inter-
fere with those who know the true nature of the work of God's

finger in the world.[4] He, Kepler, was finally opening the Book of Nature at its most secret places. It is our duty (*Aufgabe*), he writes in a letter to a correspondent, to celebrate God in the most ample manner, and the more deeply we probe, the more we recognize the grandeur of the Creation. When Kepler finally solved the problem of the orbit of Mars, he exclaimed in an ecstasy that it was as if he had grasped God with his hands.

Of all the major seventeenth-century scientists, Kepler, a passionate believer, has given the most fervid utterance to the theology of glory. He becomes so transported with his discovery and his adoration of God the designer and builder that it seems to him as if God Himself in the original creation, by working with rules and measures, had been imitating the architectural art of the human being yet to be created. The idea that the world was fashioned in accordance with pre-existing forms has many well-known philosophical and mystical origins and analogues. One is even reminded of the Cabbalist myth that God peered into the *Torah Kadumah* and molded the world in accordance with what He found in that primeval, pre-Creation Torah. (Kepler lived for many years in Prague, one of the great Cabbalist centers of Europe.) In likening God to a human architect, Kepler recognizes that man and God have the same language, the language of number and form.

Why should one engage in scientific inquiry? Kepler asks in another magnificent passage. His answer is neither mildly utilitarian in Bacon's sense, nor an expression of charity, love of one's neighbor. Kepler replies that science-making is an inherent attribute of human nature, as singing is of a bird. Science really needs no apology, says Kepler: it is a natural expression of man. In science-making, man is fulfilling his innermost being as he was created by God.

Galileo regarded mathematical knowledge as innate in man and this made it possible for him to comprehend the mathematical character of the universe. In Galileo's religious world, God is the infinitely great geometric artificer and man will *never* discover His full meaning or exhaust all the mathematical possibilities that are embedded in the universe. But through science man can at least approach a partial knowledge of God's creation. Galileo's is a glorification of God *and* man, a grand humanist vision. There is an active God, and it is the duty of the active man made in His image to pursue that portion of the truth about Him which is discoverable. Of the two books, science is the nobler expression of God. The two books are in competition, but competition for knowledge of the divine.

Time and again, in their rather detailed presentations of the differences between the Book of Nature and the Book of Scriptures, Kepler and Galileo recurred to the popular language of the Bible. In a letter to his disciple Castelli, and more particularly in a letter to the Duchess Cristina of Tuscany, as well as in passages of the great *Dialogues,* all of which were combed by the Inquisition, Galileo insisted upon an "accommodation argument" that was not necessarily heretical in the Catholic Church: The Scriptures were originally addressed to a "volgo assai rozo e indisciplinato" (a rather boorish and unruly people).[5] The emphasis upon the primitive and untutored state of the Israelites had been remarked upon in the preceding century. Galileo goes out of his way to praise Moses for his sagacity in explaining nature to ordinary people in terms of the sense of sight; but science as distinguished from Scripture was composed in a special arcane language that was differentiated from the superficial language of the senses used in everyday speech and in the Bible. To our eyes the earth seems to stand fixed in the center and the sun to circumvolve about it, just as to those shoving off from the banks of a river in a boat, the shore seems to move backward; they do not perceive that it is they who are going forward, away from the motionless shore.

Kepler had earlier made the same distinction between sense impressions and the explanations of the new philosophy. He had intended to include in the first edition of *The Cosmographic Mystery,* published in 1596, a long section arguing learnedly that his system was not contradictory to Scripture, but he had eliminated the digression on advice of his friends that he should not irritate the Lutheran consistory. In the opening of the 1609 edition of *The New Astronomy,* he threw caution to the winds and went further than Galileo later did in presenting a psychological explanation of the language employed by Moses in Genesis. Kepler makes the point that even when science finally triumphs and the basic truth of the new Copernican system, with Kepler's emendations, is accepted by everyone in the world, human beings will continue to speak about sunrise and sunset as if the sun went around the earth. "It is impossible that we should alienate our speech from this sense of our eyes."[6] Our everyday talk will continue to be shaped by our vision, even when we know the reality to be otherwise—a brilliant, psychological prophecy.

Galileo was confident that there would be an accumulation of scientific knowledge over thousands of years—a belief rare in the Renaissance despite a few phrases in Bruno and Bacon about truth being the daughter of time. "Nature, inexorable and unchanging, never transcends the limits of the laws imposed upon her, nor cares at all," he writes, "whether her recondite reasons and methods of operation are or are not exposed to the understanding of men."[7] But human effort can force from nature something of this knowledge after centuries of trial. The Catholic theologians of Galileo's day were pretending that at any given moment the Church was the repository of the totality of knowledge about nature. Galileo tried to prove that Saint Augustine himself had taken no such absolutist position. Kepler before him had already been careful to draw up a list of all the patently false scientific notions in the Church Fathers. Like the devil quoting Scripture, Galileo discovered in that acerb churchman Tertullian a passage that seemed to bestow superiority on the Book of Nature over theological doctrine. Galileo was quoting the Father for his own purposes and stretching the meaning of the original text with the skill of a clerical exegete. "We conclude," he quotes from Tertullian against Marcion, "God is known first through nature, and then again by doctrine: nature in His works; by doctrine in His revealed word."[8] In the sequence God in His works precedes the word. Throughout his polemics, Galileo, trying desperately to establish the immunity of scientists from the intervention of any other corps, especially churchmen, keeps harping upon the special language and letters in which the

Book of Nature is written, the uniqueness of its mathematical language and geometric figures. Those who do not possess this knowledge can only wander about as in a labyrinth if they venture to deal with nature.

Giorgio de Santillana has unraveled the political and ecclesiastical details of the trial of Galileo. But the heart of the matter may be less the issue of disobedience to a command of the Church, around which the formal charges centered, than the commonsense admonition that was communicated to him many times when he was still a favorite of the Church: "Keep out of the sacristy!" Neither before nor after Galileo, however, were scientists of genius willing to accept any such restriction. And it is highly questionable whether taking such a position is possible, even when the sacristy is translated into a secular moral order.

When Kepler was working for the Holy Roman Emperor he could write to Pistorius, the emperor's confessor, of his unalterable opposition to the claim that the Catholic Church had the capacity to interpret Scriptures in those passages where astronomical matters were involved. Nor would he concede any such right to his own Lutheran consistory. The dying Pistorius, who was his friend, reproved him gently: "Please leave theology out of the *Spiel*."[9] Another friend, the Lutheran divine of Tübingen Hafenreffer, cautioned him in a similar vein on February 17, 1619: "In a word, where theological matters are involved, hands off!"[10] But such discretion was alien to Kepler. He had had specific *theological* disagreements with the consistory about the nature of Christ and he could not, against his conscience, unconditionally sign the 1580 *Concordienformel* that was supposed to have affirmed the real presence of the Body of Christ in the communion of the Last Supper. Theological differences about christological matters spilled over and made him suspect in all religious questions involving Scripture. His letters and theological writings are pervaded by the belief that the real truth of God's creation, His plan in the formation of the world, which above all else reveals divine omnipotence and omniscience, was to be discovered in the Book of Nature and not in Scripture. It was in the Book of Nature that he sought an answer to the question why there was a fixed number of planets and why there were specific intervals in their orbits, which Tycho Brahe's observations had indicated. The words of Scripture, which the theologians had interpreted, afforded no such key to the underlying divine plan in the creation of the world.

At times Galileo could be even more rambunctious than Kepler. His display of a knowledge of Scripture and of the Church Fathers in his private letters and published dialogues makes it abundantly clear that to him Scripture interpretation was too grave a matter to be left to the theologians alone. The theologians were often stupid and ignorant about the character of the Book of Nature. They thought that the Book of Nature was just another book like the *Aeneid* or the *Odyssey,* and that one learned about it by writing commentaries on texts of Aristotle. In his letter to the Grand Duchess Cristina he could not refrain from quoting a naughty quip (ascribed in his notes to Cardinal Baronius): The intention of the Holy Ghost is to teach us *come se vadia al cielo*—how one goes to heaven—but not *come vadia il cielo*—how heaven goes.[11]

Galileo was willing to concede that both the Book of Nature and the Book of Scriptures were mysterious and veiled. Literal interpretations were preposterous in the analysis of either book. Galileo, like many orthodox Catholic interpreters of the Book of Scriptures before him, made a mockery of obvious anthropomorphisms in the depiction of God. And were there actual windows in heaven because the expression was used in the account of the Deluge? Nor would Galileo rest content with an allegorical interpretation of the Bible. If there were difficult phrases in those passages that referred to the natural world, then the theologians ought to turn to the scientists for help in comprehending the texts. Galileo was not afraid to propose an exegesis of Joshua's command to the sun to stand still that rendered the text completely in harmony with the Copernican hypothesis. The command to the sun to stand still was not a reference to its motion around the earth, but to the music of the spheres. Joshua was enjoining stillness, silence, upon the sun so that his voice might be the more readily heard above the din of battle.

According to Galileo, there were not two truths, even though there were two books, and vital truths about anything that concerned the natural world could be expounded only by the scientists. Even if one granted—as Galileo did—that mysteries of the Catholic Church with respect to Christ and salvation were the special province of the Church and that this knowledge was of a superior order, theologians had no business interfering in scientific matters because they had no expertise in this field, any more than they did in scores of other human occupations about which they did not presume to express opinions. Galileo had been a novice in the monastery of Vallombrosa and Kepler had studied at Tübingen to be a professor of theology before he was shunted off to teach mathematics by his superiors at the university. Scriptural exegesis was commonplace knowledge for both of them; it was science that required the extraordinary capabilities that were their special gift from God.

Galileo and Kepler both suffered for their vainglory, and their fate was a grim reminder to their contemporaries. Whenever two sources of truth, or alternative ways to the knowledge of God, are recognized, the threat of rival claims cannot be dismissed. The mutually exclusive pretensions of science and religion were never settled on the Continent, neither by Descartes's dualism nor Leibniz's universal harmony. In the next century the radical operations of Enlightenment thought exacerbated the conflict. In its fleeting moment of triumph during the French Revolution the corps of scientists imagined that the demands of revelation were silenced forever as the hypothesis of the existence of God became superfluous to a Laplace. But the two books have remained ensconced in separate spiritual bodies and the warfare of science and religion, once mocked as an illusion, may yet be rekindled with a new vigor.

IV

If the European Continental world was faced with a militant anticlerical crusade among the *philosophes* who worshiped at the altar of science, the English world inherited from Isaac Newton a very different model for the relations between science and religion. The

Royal Society, which he stamped indelibly with his personality when he served as its autocratic president for more than a quarter of a century, upheld the ideal of the neutrality of science in public affairs, while in the private person of the scientist an intimate union of science and religion was achieved that weathered the Enlightenment and was not seriously questioned in the English-speaking world until the controversies engendered by the Darwinian theory. Newton the believer became the prototypical figure of English and American science.

The persecutions Kepler and Galileo endured were unthinkable in England of the Restoration. By the time Newton came up to Cambridge in the early 1660s, the English world had moved into a totally different religious and scientific atmosphere. The Anglican Church not only tolerated science, but espoused its works and honored its practitioners. Literally scores of scientists earned their living as clergymen and wrote works of theology. As for the two most notable figures of the age, Boyle and Newton, though they never took orders, they lived ascetic lives and conceived of both their scientific and religious works as glorifications of God.

Despite the murkiness of some of Newton's religious expressions over the years—and many of them were not philosophically felicitous, even with his disciple the Reverend Samuel Clarke as a mouthpiece—some things can be asserted. He never upheld a simple mechanistic view of the universe, nor was he a partisan of plain Deistic natural religion. It may be wicked to quote the devil on the God of Isaac Newton when there are so many pious bishops to bear witness, but Voltaire's report, after conversations with Clarke, has the virtues of clarity and brevity: "Sir Isaac Newton was firmly persuaded of the Existence of a God; by which he understood not only an infinite, omnipotent, and creating being, but moreover a Master who has made a Relation between himself and his Creatures."[12] The world was not eternal. Creation was a specific act in time by a Lord, even though the process of His labors was perhaps more complex than the popular notion of the Mosaic account in Genesis. The planets had to be distributed in a particular manner by an initial act before the principle of gravity could become operative. They were then slowly accelerated from a state of inertia. Comets were phenomena in whose progress God had to intervene from time to time. A repeopling of the earth after major geological or cosmic catastrophes—and there may have been such incidents in the past—required a divine decree. And as the world had a beginning, there was likely to be an apocalyptic end. Every discovery of a scientific principle of matter, every correct reading of a prophetic text, demonstrated the essential goodness and orderliness of the universe that God had created. What higher praise could be uttered by the religious philosopher?

When Newton was named to the Royal Society in 1672, discoveries about God's world had begun to mount up at an accelerated pace. A monotheistic culture must inevitably become engaged in the search for a unifying principle, and can never remain content with the mere amassing of isolated findings and inventions, astonishing as they may be. Newton represents the fulfillment of that quest for underlying unity. "Without Gravity, the whole Universe . . . would have been a confused Chaos,"[13] lectured Richard Bentley in the first noteworthy popularization of Newton's laws. The Newtonian system, with its mathematically described force that applied both to the movements of the heavenly bodies and to things on earth, came to satisfy a religious as well as a scientific need. In achieving the great synthesis with a law that showed the interrelationship of all parts of creation, at the very moment when it seemed as if science might remain an agglomeration of curiosities and disparate discoveries—Hooke's, Boyle's, Marcello Malpighi's—Newton overwhelmed his fellow scientists, and became the symbol of science in a Christian society.

Some of Newton's theological manuscripts were once shown to Albert Einstein. Despite the fact that it was September 1940, the eve of his involvement with an apocalyptic enterprise of his own, he took the trouble to compose a letter appreciating the papers for the insight they afforded into Newton's *geistige Werkstatt*, his "spiritual workshop."[14] On the other hand, George Sarton, that prodigious innovator in the history of science, expressed cool indifference: "I am a scientist and no more interested in Newton's non-mathematical works than a medical man would be in the rabbinical books of Maimonides."[15] Such has been the polarity of modern responses to Isaac Newton the theologian.

Most of Newton's manuscripts on religion were long concealed from the world. In 1729, shortly after his death, the rejected disciple William Whiston reprinted in a little pamphlet a few "Quaeries" to the Optics, the General Scholium of later editions of the *Principia*, and scattered bits from the *Chronology of Ancient Kingdoms Amended:* in toto a paltry thirty-one pages that Newton had himself published on religion.[16] The *Observations upon the Prophecies of Daniel and the Apocalypse of St. John* was put together in 1733 by his nephew Benjamin Smith, a dilettante-cleric not renowned for his piety—this was an insignificant selection from a vast archive at his disposal. For two hundred years thereafter, the remaining manuscripts were suppressed, bowdlerized, sequestered, or neglected, lest what were believed to be shady lucubrations tarnish the image of the perfect scientific genius.

In the Sotheby sale of the Portsmouth Collection in 1936, Newton's nonscientific manuscripts were strewn about rather haphazardly. But since that date, most of them have been reassembled and are in safe keeping, thanks to the zeal of an improbable trio, an eminent British economist, an American stockmarket analyst, and a Yale professor. Special collections in Cambridge (England), Wellesley, and Jerusalem now bear the names of Keynes, Babson, and Yahuda respectively. Isolated papers still turn up occasionally; and there are documents from the Royal Mint (in the Public Record Office) in which accounts of the coinage are interspersed with reflections on the Gnostics and the Cabbala. For the first time since the great dispersion, virtually everything that Newton wrote on religion is freely available.

Though in his old age Newton committed numerous documents to the flames, he spared a dissertation exposing as false the trinitarian proof texts in John and Timothy and scores of other theological writings, more than a million words. There are extant four separate commentaries on Daniel and the Apocalypse, a church history complete in multiple versions, rules for reading the lan-

guage of the prophets, many drafts of an Irenicum, a treatise on
the years of Christ's preaching, and extensive notes on Christian
heresies through the ages—all this in addition to hundreds of
pages of excerpts from contemporary works of scholarly divinity,
Latin translations of the Talmud, and the writings of the Church
Fathers, to say nothing of papers that appear to be related to Samuel Clarke's replies to Leibniz.

Even a cursory examination of the manuscripts excludes any
bifurcation of Newton's life into a robust youth and manhood,
when he performed experiments, adhered to rigorous scientific
method, and wrote the *Principia,* and a dotage during which he
wove mystical fantasies and occupied himself with the Book of
Daniel and the Apocalypse of Saint John—a legend first propagated by the French astronomer Jean-Baptiste Biot in the early
nineteenth century. Some of the livelier versions of Newton's commentaries on prophecy should be dated to the 1670s and 1680s,
when he was in his prime. His studies of world chronology and
philosophical alchemy, both linked to his theology, began early
in his Cambridge years and continued until his death.

In Newton's interpretation of the history of the Church, the
original formula of Christian belief, "milk for babes," was contained in a few phrases about God the Creator, Christ, and the Resurrection taken directly out of Scripture. Any later deviations
were corruptions. In an ideal Christian polity anyone who subscribed to the primitive apostolic creed—"short and free from
repetitions as a symbol of religion ought to be . . . easy to be
understood and remembered by the common people," Newton
said[17]—was not to be excluded from the communion or in any
way persecuted, no matter what other religious opinions he might
hold.

Parallels to many of Newton's antitrinitarian arguments can
be found in the voluminous writings of contemporaries—Samuel
Clarke and William Whiston, the avowed unitarian Thomas Em-
lyn, the humanitarian Hopton Haynes, and Socinian Samuel
Crell. These men had a common treasury well stocked with biblical quotations, and Newton ploughed through their works and

the frequent episcopal refutations they provoked. But he invariably tried to find his own way. It would be an error to seize upon his antitrinitarianism in order to pigeonhole him in one of the recognized categories of heresy—Arian, Socinian, Unitarian, or Deist. On many christological questions, he never settled into a fixed position. While his villain in the history of the Church was Athanasius rather than Arius, he censured both for having introduced metaphysical subtleties and confusion into the plain language of Scripture. (In the light of modern scholarship his Athanasius is a rather imaginary figure, having long since been denied authorship of the creed to which his name is attached.)

Newton went to great pains to distinguish his private beliefs about the nature of Christ from both those held by trinitarians and those held by the unorthodox who conceived of Him as a mere man. The arguments he used have a personal flavor, even though they are hardly revolutionary innovations in heterodox Christology. The phrase "the man Christ Jesus," which appears in Newton's manuscripts many times, should not be pulled out of context to impute to him an eighteenth-century Deistic view that identified Christ as merely another prophet or an inspired human being. Christ had assumed and would assume many shapes and forms spiritual and physical as a Saviour, a messenger, an agent, a vice-ruler under God, a judge, a human being. Christ was the Messiah and the Son of God; and after the Resurrection, it was Christ who would prepare heavenly mansions for the elect in a remote part of the universe.

Anything that appeared to derogate from the absolute dominion and supreme monarchy of God the Father was repugnant to Newton. The Holy Ghost was simply the spirit of prophecy. And though Christ was the Lamb of God prayers were to be directed to "God in the name of the Lamb, but not to the Lamb in the name of God."[18] Unlike Samuel Clarke, Newton left behind no revised Anglican Prayer-Book and service with every trinitarian passage slashed through with violent penstrokes—the book is preserved in the British Museum—but he would have agreed in principle with most of the deletions and substitutions, which in each instance stressed obedience to one God owed by men as His servants and diminished the other two persons of the Trinity.

But if the role of Christ in Newton's theology was far from orthodox, and if in his history of the Church he continually reiterated his antitrinitarian beliefs, why did he not stand up and fight along with William Whiston against every alien phrase insinuated by the Anglican Church into the primitive apostolic creed? Why did he not join the "Society for the Restoration of Primitive Christianity" that Whiston had founded? After Newton's death Hopton Haynes, who had worked under him at the Mint for decades, criticized him in private for not having heeded the call to lead a reformation in the Church equal to that of Luther and Calvin; and Whiston, who was ousted from the Lucasian chair as an Arian heretic, in his memoirs accused Newton of religious duplicity.

Was Newton hypocritical? Was he afraid? Had he succumbed to the fleshpots when he became Master of the Mint and President of the Royal Society? The divine Newton, it would seem, was all too human. But there were cogent reasons for Newton's refusal to throw in his lot with Whiston. Newton faced the eternal dilemma of all dissenters within a religious or political communion: to submit, gloss over differences, remain silent for the sake of unity, or to listen to the voice of conscience and proclaim a particular truth come what may. Beliefs were changing. There would come a time, he told John Conduitt, when trinitarian doctrines hallowed by the Church would be considered as outlandish as Catholic transubstantiation. Why raise tumults against an evil whose day was passing? The punishments that could be meted out to a man who published antitrinitarian views were harsh. And apart from simple motives of preserving comfort and status and tranquillity, Newton's manuscripts prove that he had authentic, deeply felt, irenical convictions, which had first been nourished by the Cambridge Platonists and were then reinforced during the years of his friendship with John Locke.

Newton's considered public reticence and the toleration preached in his Irenic manuscripts should not, however, mislead us about the animosity that pervades his histories of corruption in the Church. These are profuse, vituperative, and, in their attacks on persons, relentless. Commitment to a latitudinarian spirit was one thing; silence in the face of deliberate distortion of plain scriptural truth and the introduction of metaphysical concepts in the guise of religion was another matter.

The corrupters of religion, ancient and modern, were legion: the contemporary Papists and their antecedents, the pagan idolaters; the English sectarian enthusiasts—the new prophets—and their equivalents, the hallucinating monks of early Christianity; the Pharisaical Jews who rejected Christ; contemporary Deists and atheists like Hobbes and their ancient counterparts the theological Epicureans, for whom all was chance; and finally, the philosophers who mixed up metaphysics and religion, particularly the modern rationalist system-makers Descartes and Leibniz, and their predecessors the Gnostics, Cabbalists, and Platonists. These were the enemies of Newton's God.

A fragment entitled "Of the faith which was once delivered to the Saints," in which Newton excoriated the old corrupters of the Christian religion for insinuating metaphysical interpretations and principles into the Church, has passages that anticipate and virtually paraphrase sections of the General Scholium in the second edition of the *Principia* (1713): "If God be called ʽο παντοκρά-τωρ the omnipotent, they take it in a metaphysical sense for Gods power of creating all things out of nothing whereas it is meant principally of his universal irresistible monarchical power to teach us obedience. . . . If the father or son be called *God,* they take the name in a metaphysical sense as if it signified Gods metaphysical perfections of infinite eternal omniscient omnipotent whereas it relates only to Gods dominion to teach us obedience."[19] The argument that God is a Master, that men have a personal relationship to a Lord, not to abstract attributes, was transplanted by Newton from ancient to modern times, from considerations of early church history to polemics in the General Scholium, bearing with it his virulent antimetaphysical bias, one of the constants of his religious and scientific outlook. Metaphysics was an evil to be combated because this mode of thinking—system-making, building hypothetical structures—was pre-eminently responsible for the perversion of the only truly revealed religion, primitive Christianity.

The modern philosophical system-makers were acting precisely as had the ancient Platonists, Gnostics, and Cabbalists. Instead of concentrating upon God's works, His actions, the phenomena, as a form of worship, they were presuming a knowledge of His attributes or His essence. Leibniz was Athanasius *redivivus*. Supermundane intelligences, pre-established harmonies, were hypotheses of the same order as the Cabbalist *sephirot*, Plato's *logos*, and Simon Magus's foul emanations.

While Leibniz and his cohorts were plaguing Newton for having posited a universe that was not perfect in itself and required God's intervention from time to time, Newton glorified those very interventions as the supreme acts of God's providential will. God had constantly intervened in the history of the physical world: in creating it through a subordinate spiritual agent who was probably Jesus in one of His many manifestations, and in creating it in one way rather than in another; in preserving and sustaining the world; and in directing comets one way rather than another. And He would possibly do other things to the physical world, perhaps burn it and start life over again on some other planet, perhaps leave a remnant and renew life on the same planet. God had also intervened continually in the history of mankind, restoring true religion after successive lapses among both Jews and Christians. The whole creation and all of history were interventions.

For Newton intervention did not imply physical or historical chaos. There were underlying operational designs in the world that could be defined as the history of the motions of the planets, which displayed a marvelous orderliness, and the history of the revolutions of empires and churches, which had a similarly simple pattern—one so simple that it could be contained in two small books, Daniel and the Apocalypse, that were really repetitions of each other.

The history of the world was epitomized in books of prophecy—hence the centrality of commentaries on prophecy in Newton's scriptural and historical religion. The prophet was a religious teacher chosen by God as a vehicle of Revelation because of his hard-won rational perfections, not his unbridled flights of fantasy. He was no hot enthusiast. It was the *language* of prophecy that was obscure and veiled; the mind of the prophet was pellucid in its clarity, precise and parsimonious in its expression of the Holy Spirit. The meaning of prophecy was concealed, as were the laws of nature, that other book in which God had written a record of His actions; and Newton drew frequent parallels between unraveling the mysteries of the books of prophecy and discovering the secrets of the Book of Nature. That the complete content of prophecy had been hidden until the seventeenth century was for Newton "nothing but what ought to have been."[20] And perhaps with a touch of circularity he reasoned that the very circumstance of his revealing in his commentaries the fullness of prophecy was a sign that the consummation of the times was not far distant.

It is understandable that Newton should have turned to Daniel and John as the preferred prophets—their enigmatic symbols and images were a challenge, the baffling episodes and visions demanded explanation. God's communication of these words to two chosen prophets was an historical act that made no sense whatever unless it was intended that their meaning would ultimately be deciphered. "If they are never to be understood, to what end did God reveale them?" Newton asked in a manuscript of the early Cambridge period.[21]

Newton worked out a dictionary of historical, political, and ecclesiastical equivalents for the images and symbols in prophetic literature. His presumption was that prophecies were congruent in all their parts without fault or exception. Once an appropriate political translation of any given "prophetic hieroglyph" (the phrase is Newton's) had been determined, that same meaning had to apply whenever it appeared in a book of prophecy. The tests of truth were constancy and consistency. Newton showed not only that every notable political and religious occurrence in history had been foretold in some vision in prophecy, if correctly understood, but that his set of equivalents had totally exhausted the possible meaning of each of the objects and images appearing in any prophetic verse. There were none left over, no random words still unexplained, no images that were superfluous. The system was closed, complete, and flawless.

In manuscripts of his early Cambridge years on the millennium and the "world-to-come," Newton gave expression to a theology of glory in effusive language. There was genuine, almost rhapsodic, wonderment at the complex and infinite powers of the Creator:

He that shall well consider the strange and wonderful nature of life and the frame of Animals, will think nothing beyond the possibility of nature, nothing too hard for the omnipotent power of God. And as the Planets remain in their orbs, so may any other bodies subsist at any distance from the earth, and much more may beings, who have a sufficient power of self motion, move whether they will, place themselves where they will, and continue in any regions of the heavens whatever, there to enjoy the society of one another, and by their messengers or Angels to rule the earth and convers with the remotest regions. . . . And to have thus the liberty and dominion of the whole heavens and the choice of the happiest places for abode seems a greater happiness then to be confined to any one place whatever.[22]

This from a man who hardly ever ventured beyond the Woolsthorpe, Cambridge, London triangle.

In such passages Newton successfully communicates his sense of the presence of invisible things and his awed amazement at the plenitude of the creation. His universe is a plenum of spiritual beings, and this may help to account for his opposition to the idea of a material plenum. This man of the melancholy countenance, as Henry More described him, seemed to fancy himself soaring through the heavens. The prospect of moving through vast spaces did not terrify him—they would be filled with a happy throng of saintly companions, as in many a Church Father's description of paradise. Alas, in the manuscripts he prepared during his last years I find no such poetic transports. When the aging Newton was the autocrat of British science and Master of the Royal Mint, he copied and edited and abstracted and emended his apocalyptic interpretations, until they turned into an arid chronicle of political and ecclesiastical events. The fonts of creativity had dried up in science and in religion.

Newton's statement of fundamental religious principles, his interpretation of prophecy, his textual criticism of the historical works of Scripture, his system of world chronology, his cosmological theories, and his Euhemeristic reduction of pagan mythology all bespeak the same mentality and style of thought. As nature was consonant with itself, so was Isaac Newton's mind. At the height of his powers there was in him a compelling drive to find order and design in what appeared to be chaos, to distill from a vast inchoate mass of materials a few basic principles that would embrace the whole and define the relationships of its component parts.

Newton could not rest content with merely contemplating the sheer variety and multiplicity of historical events, any more than he could a world of disparate observations about nature. In whatever direction he turned, he was searching for a unifying structure. He tried to force everything in the heavens and on earth into a rigid, tight frame from which the most minuscule detail could not escape.

Whatever knowledge of God was revealed in the Book of Scriptures was harmonious with what was unfolded in the Book of Nature. A manuscript on rules for interpreting prophecy dwells on the similarity between the goals of the scientist and of the prophecy expositor, and discloses in stark language that an identical quest for simplicity and unity underlay Newton's researches into both books. "Truth," Newton wrote,

is ever to be found in simplicity, and not in the multiplicity and confusion of things. As the world, which to the naked eye exhibits the greatest variety of objects, appears very simple in its internall constitution when surveyed by a philosophic understanding, and so much the simpler by how much the better it is understood, so it is in these [prophetic] visions. It is the perfection of God's works that they are all done with the greatest simplicity. He is the God of order and not of confusion. And therefore as they that would understand the frame of the world must indeavour to reduce their knowledg to all possible simplicity, so it must be in seeking to understand these visions.[23]

All of Newton's studies were animated by one overwhelming desire, to know God's will through His works in the world.

Throughout the Enlightenment, whenever scriptural arguments were raised among Christian believers who would have their science and their Bible too, the rhetorics of Kepler, Galileo, and Newton were revived in hundreds of different forms, with or without ascription to the eminent scientists. Their hermeneutics and exegesis of specific biblical texts eased the acceptance of science among the orthodox and at the same time the scientists came to serve as bulwarks against disbelief. If religion was acceptable to such magnificent representatives of the rational capacity, who are you, little man, to continue to parade your puny doubts? The wonders of the God of Kepler, Galileo, and above all Newton, revealed in the Book of Nature, could sway some believers of a new age as profoundly as the God of Abraham, Isaac, and Jacob who had recorded His commandments in the Book of Scriptures.

2 DEISTS ON TRUE AND FALSE GODS

Primitive monotheism, the orthodox theory among both Catholics and Protestants, was assimilated into the system of natural religion evolved by the followers of Lord Herbert of Cherbury, though the heterodox glosses they insinuated were far from palatable either to the highly ritualistic or to the enthusiastic branches of Christianity. The Deist view of the origin of religion was propagated by a wide variety of writers, many of them bitterly inimical to one another, ranging from the pantheist John Toland through respectable Anglican cathedral deans with a penchant for rationality in religion. The ideas were by no means exclusively English. Respectable abbés like Charles Le Batteux could subscribe to a Deist-like adaptation of the dogma of primitive monotheism colored by the eighteenth-century philosophical spirit and still remain in the Académie des Inscriptions et Belles-Lettres. Voltaire had imported the doctrine into France along with the rest of the Deist philosophy and later defended it against the Holbachian atheists in *Dieu et les hommes, oeuvre théologique mais raisonnable, par le docteur Obern* (1769), which by order of the Parlement was consumed in the same flames as the *Système de la nature*. Diderot found primitive monotheism wholly acceptable, at least in the mood of the *Essai sur le mérite et la vertu* (1745) and *De la suffisance de la religion naturelle* (1747). German professors of Göttingen like Johann Mosheim had a natural affinity for the religious theory of their fellow subjects of the Hanoverian dynasty, though they would never have identified themselves as Deists. The Germans of the *Aufklärung* who reduced religion to morality— Gotthold Ephraim Lessing, Johann August von Starck, and Christoph Meiners—were in the same school, demystifying all religions, identifying their common rationality, equating the *lex rationis* and the *lex naturae* with revelation. But despite the profuse Continental imitations, Deism retained a predominantly English flavor, and its treatment of nonrationalist religious manifestations was unique, and somewhat parochial.

I

The English Deists were especially favored by the political circumstances of the period immediately following the Glorious Revolution. The new monarchy wanted neither fanatic Puritans nor miracle-making Papists about—it looked to an orderly, sober church establishment. The line of tolerance was still drawn at atheism or at a denial of the divinity of Christ, but for the most part this was an open society in which religious controversy was permitted in high places. The intellectual temper was in many respects freer than it was later in the century. Deism in England had its poverty-stricken, vain, boisterous, hapless, uncontrollable pamphleteers, but it also enjoyed prestige and power in the realm, for among its adepts were great lords and gentlemen, Shaftesbury, Bolingbroke, Anthony Collins, Charles Blount. Only in England had the separation of church and state proceeded so far that disputants could engage in open theological debate without jeopardizing their personal libery, interpret biblical texts loosely, and discuss miracles and the psychology of religion with impunity. Englishmen did not need to expose the impostures of pagan oracles as a subterfuge when their real target was ritualistic Judaism and Christianity. There were occasional threats from the attorney-general and a measure of self-censorship among publishers, but there was no Bastille.

The major problems confronting a Deist in the reconstruction of a world history of religion had already been faced by the orthodox. How explain the bewildering variety of religious experience, which the voyage literature and translations from the Chinese, Indian, Persian, and Vedic sacred writings had thrust into the forefront of European consciousness? How account for the startling conformities among heathens ancient and modern and the even more disturbing fact that pagan rituals and beliefs showed marked resemblances to the Judaic and Christian revelations and ceremonial practices? Why had God allowed monstrous perversions of His pure Being to exist in the world? By 1700 a body of traditional solutions had been accumulated in Christendom that satisfied the pious. Savage cult objects and rituals that had counterparts in Christianity were, after momentary dismay, neatly enlisted as proofs of true religion. The barbaric rite was a remnant of the primitive monotheism of Adam, a corruption that still preserved enough of the authentic revelation to resemble the original; or it was a prefiguration of the truth that was to be announced, crude in form, but a foretelling, like the words of the Old Testament prophets and the utterances of the sibyls; or it was an early usage that God, out of condescension, because it was harmless and amenable to a Christian interpretation, allowed to be metamorphosed into a sacrament. Maimonides had used the same conception to justify the continuation of paganlike sacrifices under Mosaic law. Conformities among savage idolatries themselves were easy to explain through the patristic demonological doctrine. The same demons were operative in all paganisms; these seducers of mankind were incapable of novelty and were repetitive. The noncreative demons, the apes of God, could only imitate and corrupt with slight variations the one true religious tradition, which had a continuous history from Adam through Christ.

The eighteenth-century Deists rejected the demonolgy, the condescension, and the prefiguration as crude anthropomorphisms, and set out in search of fresh naturalistic interpretations, though many of the older religious motifs are still discernible beneath the new vestments.

The belief that there was some common denominator in all religious manifestations had been growing among Europeans since the discoveries of the New World. What Calvin in the *Institutes* recognized as a glimmer of truth in the darkness of paganism became the Deist natural religion embodied in different forms and shapes. Ralph Cudworth's *True Intellectual System of the Universe* (1678) expressed enlightened English Protestant theory in his day. "Having treated largely concerning the Two most eminent Polytheists among the ancient Pagans, Zoroaster and Orpheus, and clearly proved that they asserted One Supreme Deity; we shall in the next place observe, that the Egyptians themselves also, notwithstanding their Multifarious *Polytheisms* and Idolatry, had an acknowledgement, amongst them, of one Supreme, and Universal Numen."[1] Primitive Christianity, the unadorned teachings of Christ, was the essence of religion in all times and places, universally admitted. When the seventeenth-century Jesuits allowed ancient Chinese formulas such as "Adore the Heavens" to remain in the temples of their new converts, they were unwittingly bolstering a form of universal Deism, and the Dominicans were quick to warn the Papacy of this latitudinarian danger. If the Jesuits could presume that the Chinese mandarins had reached the halfway mark toward Christianity, why should Greek and Roman philosophical authors, whose profound moral sentiments were the education of Europe, be denied a knowledge of one God? The ancient pagans could offer no resistance to their ex post facto conversion to Deist Christianity. What the Jesuits did for the Chinese, the philosophical divines of the Anglican Church accomplished for the more worthy philosophers among the Greeks, the Romans, and the Egyptians. The prospect was opened up for these religious English humanists that some day in another sphere they might have converse in the groves of academe with Cicero, Seneca, and Plutarch, perhaps even with Socrates himself.

Most Deists were far more interested in proving that man was naturally a religious animal than in exalting the special character of Christian revelation. The religious debate had been transferred to another level: The problem was no longer to show the superiority of Christianity over Judaism and Mohammedanism or the truth of a particular Christian sect, but to defend religion itself against the libertine argument that it was not necessary to man. Even for orthodox Catholics it had become more important to demonstrate that the most benighted savage, that a wild found-ling discovered crawling in the woods, had a natural inkling of God than to win a battle over theological niceties. Inevitably, in the course of the facile conversion of American savages, Chinese mandarins, and Greek polytheists to primitive monotheism, the traditionalist Christians bent their dogma more than a little in the direction of Deist conceptions whose name they would have abhorred.

Despite John Locke's famous refutation of the innate idea of God in the *Essay Concerning Human Understanding* (1690), even those Deists who accepted his general epistemology clung to the notion that man was created with a religious spark in his bosom, an inborn sentiment that was in content virtually equivalent to the moral principles of a Christian English Deist circa 1700. Original man was a benign creature, ever prone as an instinctive impulse of his being to love his brethren and to worship the Deity who created the world. The quintessential nature of man, constant in his devotion to God, beneficent and pionus, was identical throughout time. In his effusions of kindness and gratitude to God for the bountiful nature that sustained him, he acted spontaneously, but he was also a rational creature who comprehended the natural order and the philosophical justification for his sentiments. Arguments from design fortified his primitive monotheism. This tender man, loving and reasonable, religious and sociable, needed no positive law to guide him and required no sacerdotal establishments to prescribe forms of worship, since adoration was a natural emanation of his being. "The most antient Egyptians, Persians, and Romans, the first Patriarchs of the Hebrews, with several other Nations and Sects," wrote John Toland in the *Letters to Serena* (1704), "had no sacred Images or Statues, no peculiar Places or costly Fashions of Worship; the plain Easiness of their Religion being most agreeable to the Simplicity of the Divine Nature, as indifference of Place or Time were the best expressions of infinite Power and Omnipresence."[2] Ritual was superfluous and artificial—some Deists said mechanical. When allowed free expression, natural religion manifested itself in simple, intimate, joyful praise, accompanied by symbolic gifts. This Deist idyll was a composite of images from classical Arcadia and the Garden of Eden before the Fall, crowned with the idea of innate reasonableness.

But the contradictions between this ideal of natural religion and the ugly realities of religious experience familiar to the most casual observer of world history cried out for conciliation. What had happened to defile the purity of natural religion? How did mankind fall from the rational precepts and natural sentiments related to primitive monotheism into the abyss of the more vulgar positive religions? Man had the mind to conceive of a Supreme Being; he knew through his natural benevolence the basic moral precepts of love toward fellow men and thankfulness toward God. What then had corrupted him? The eruption of idolatrous behavior sometime in remote antiquity—the precise date was in controversy—was readily recognized by the Fathers as a symptom of evil and original sin, but the rationalist Deists could not resort to such supernatural explanations. In tracing the history of religious decline from pure primitive monotheism, the Deists were constrained to invent a commonsense rationale for the growth of the multifarious burdensome superstitious ceremonials of all organized priesthoods, among the heathen, savage and civil, in Judaism, and in Christianity; to offer historical or at least psychological causes for the abominable rituals that were a disgrace to human dignity, for anthropomorphic idolatry and brute-worship; and to explain the pollution of what was originally the adoration of a benign God with bloody sacrifices of animals and fellow men.

As a way out of their quandary, the Deists had recourse to general reflections on human nature that rendered the naïve, bland portrait of early man more complex. True, man was created with innate religious virtues, but he was born also with natural frailty. Wherever the orthodox said sin, the Deists substituted feebleness and disease. Wherever the Puritans had thundered depravity, the Deists dolefully described error, a failure of the mechanism of true perceptions, a disorder of the senses, a confusion in the brain. Human reason, though it could grasp the truth, was weak; it could not hold it firmly; other aspects of man's nature—his imagination, his concupiscence—led him astray, so that he was lost as in a labyrinth of uncontrolled passions.

The doctrine of frailty assumed alternative forms. One posited human debility as equal in all times and places, thus preserving the predominant Deist ahistorical temper. A less frequent variant allowed that there had been a measure of change in mankind, that in the first ages human reason had been peculiarly susceptible to distortions, since like a child's brain the fibers were then very tender, a theory that led the Deists into the progressist camp where they did not ordinarily belong, for they had to conceive of a strengthening or modification of the rational tissues in time. A third possibility was perhaps the most commonly accepted of all; it entailed not one fall, one momentous degeneration, but a whole series of injuries to the reason of man, followed by periodic natural recuperation after the ministrations of great spiritual leaders who were, so to speak, the doctors of humanity, who from time to time set men's erring intellects aright with the fresh elucidation of the truths of primitive monotheism and natural religion. These religious guides had appeared at intervals in various parts of the world, and as the readings of the sacred texts of Jews, Mohammedans, Persians, Indians, and Chinese attested, they always preached the same gospel, albeit in diverse forms. Differences among the holy writings of East and West could be brushed aside as superficial local variations responsive to climatic conditions. Beneath the apparent confusion of creeds the same uniform religious principles, which had never been altered since Creation, endured.

Since most English Deists were also Christians, they were willing to allow for one exception in this history of religious reaffirmation—the revelation of Jesus, superior in its formulation of truth to all other teachings throughout the world. Over the precise quality of the uniqueness of the Christian dispensation violent theological controversy raged, and there was a whole spectrum of variegated opinion from the natural religion of respected Anglican bishops to Anthony Collins the "free-thinker." For some Deists the Christ was still a divine revelation sui generis; for others

His preachments merely differed in their degree of excellence from what had been received among the Hindus, the Chinese, the American savages. "Christianity as Ancient as the World," Tindal announced. For his followers Christ's message did not vary in its essence from the natural knowledge of God with which Adam had been endowed; it was a republication of the truth, not a new discovery; it was the most perfect of the versions, not an entirely novel revelation to mankind. It was not always clear whether in the future there would be further editions of natural religion or whether the teachings of Jesus would stand for all time as the most complete. Certainly many English Deists conceived of themselves as restorers of primitive Christianity.

The true God of the Deisis was never a God of fear and trembling, of punishment and damnation. Though Herbert of Cherbury's Deism included immortality among the five principles of religion, the previews of the hereafter were conspicuously lacking in scenes of fire and brimstone. In positive priestly religions, pagan as well as Christian, the idea of a rational God had been grossly distorted into a monstrous image of vengeance, gloating over human suffering, demanding victims. Deism, which was the original primitive monotheism, had been perverted. Into the same ignominious company should be thrust a savage American devil-worship, a Greek Zeus with his thunderbolts, a Chinese monster-god, and a Christian fanatic's God of eternal hellfire.

II

Qua historians of ancient pagan religion, many of these good Deists were driven by their insight into human weakness to propound a "twofold philosophy," a doctrine that serves to identify them beyond their common preaching of sweet reasonableness and natural religion. The formula of the double truth had been lying about in the classical corpus and needed only to be adapted and embroidered with historical evidence to resolve the apparent internal contradictions of pagan, Judaic, and even Christian practice recorded in the religious annals of mankind. At no time in human history, the theory asserted, among no people, had the belief in primitive monotheism been totally eradicated, despite the universal prevalence of idolatries and bestial popular rites. What had happened was that one group of men in a society, usually the stronger in some sense, often an organized corps, had monopolized the monotheist doctrine, transforming it into a mystery, which they veiled from the people. The initiatory ceremonies of all ancient cults preserved the truths of natural religion in a secret hieroglyphic and symbolic language.

In one form or another the double truth doctrine was entertained by episcopal worthies like Bishop William Warburton, avowed pantheists like Toland, cautious philosophical skeptics like Hume, grand Deist lords like Bolingbroke, abbés like Le Batteux, scholarly authors who specialized in the mystery cults like the Baron de Sainte-Croix, that most outrageous materialist Dr. Julien Offray de La Mettrie, the popular orthodox scientific writer Abbé Noël-Antoine Pluche, the revolutionary atheist Charles Dupuis. Wherever a sounding is made, one comes upon the idea that there were always two pagan religions: gross polytheism, with human sacrifices, brute-worship, even cabbage-worship, for the masses; secret monotheism, a religion of virtue, love, adoration of the First Cause, for an elite.

The eighteenth-century writers were obviously projecting their own religious problems and solutions back into antiquity. These elegant aristocrats of England, university men from Scotland, worldly *philosophes* in Paris, the capital of the universe, materialist doctors in Frederick II's court knew that religious ceremonials, rites, and the power of organized clergies were not necessary for their own understanding of science and nature and the rational First Cause; and yet beyond the gates of their academies and salons was a howling mob, attracted by nothing but childish superstitions. The mob followed the fanatic dissenters, the Methodist preachers, the miracles of the Abbé François de Pâris; it adored the painted dolls in Neapolitan churches and worshiped saints like idols. It was this realization that informed David Hume's *Natural History of Religion*. His contemporaries the papist idolaters and the fanatical believers in the Jansenist miracles were no different from the most vulgar primitive polytheists. There had been men of sense in antiquity, Socrates, Epicurus, Lucretius, and there was a handful of men in his own day capable of spiritual abstractions, Hume himself and his moralist friends, his antecedents Shaftesbury and Bayle and Bolingbroke. There were two religions in every society, one for the men of reason and one for the fanatics, one for those who comprehended the marvelous order of the world and one for those who still relied on gods for every event, the ignorant men full of terrors, which they allayed with ludicrous rituals.

The Humean doctrine had been preached fifty years earlier by John Toland, a magnificent stylist whose pungent writings in Latin or in translations from the English dominated the Continental debate for more than a century. For his equals, the philosophers, he wrote a service to be performed behind closed doors, *Praise to the All*. Hymns were to be chanted to free inquiry, to knowledge and truth, but only after the servants had left the banquet as in antiquity. The common herd could not understand the mysteries, neither in ancient times nor in modern. "We shall be in Safety," he wrote in the *Pantheisticon, sive formula celebrandae sodalitatis Socraticae* (1720), "if we separate ourselves from the Multitude; for the Multitude is a Proof of what is worst."[3] The mass was credulous, and since the Deists had joined ranks in a war against credulity they were often involved in a war against the people. The wise men of all time, hierophants of the mystery religions, formed a sort of esoteric brotherhood, which throughout the ages had taught the same pantheism and identical Pythagorean astronomy—"or to speak with the Moderns the Copernican"—all equally incomprehensible to the mob. The ancient mysteries were a necessary barrier before the ignorant, creating a pathos of distance to preserve truth, "inasmuch as all Philosophy is divided by the Pantheists, as well as other antient Sages, into External, or popular and depraved; and Internal, or pure and genuine."[4] The theory was not new in England. Ralph Cudworth in 1678 had already described the simultaneous existence among the Egyptians, the Persians, and the Indians of a "Vulgar and Fabulous Theory and an Arcane and Recondite Theology," but Toland made a program of action out of the doctrine.

Toland looked upon the people as children to be humored, and unwittingly contributed to the literature that assimilated the infantile, the primitive, the mad, and the superstitious. "Wherefore the Pantheists, Persons of the strictest Moderation, behave Towards frantic, foolish, and stubborn Men, as fond Nurses do towards their babbling Minions, who imbibe from them the pleasing Infatuation of imagining themselves Kings and Queens, that they are only Papa and Mama's Pets, and that there are none so pretty and so finy as they. Those who flatter not Infants in these Trifles are odious and disagreeable to them."[5] In militant Deists like Toland the fear of the mob sometimes acquired a passionate tone. The ancient founders of mysteries had rightly secreted their truths from the blind masses; in fact, the wise elite in all ages would probably have to subscribe to the double truth doctrine, allowing the common people to wallow in their superstitious corruptions of primitive monotheism while the select few communicated their natural truths to one another. Toland's despair, though not generally normative for Deist philosophy, was a current of thought that ran deep in some segments of this school. In his bitter pamphlets he denounced a condition of ecclesiastical society that forced him, a free Christian, to avail himself of a heathen practice, but there was no choice.

Warburton, the bishop with a mace spiked with learning, which he wildly heaved about him against the Tolands and the Tindals, somehow found himself plucking from their doctrinal vineyards. This "rather knock-kneed giant of theology," in one of the most confused yet remarkably influential works of the great religious controversy, ended up by demonstrating to any commonsense reader not "the divine legation of Moses" but the twofold philosophy. In the Egyptian mysteries the priests taught monotheism, future rewards and punishments. Only the ignorant peasants enmeshed in error and trapped by the deceits of their masters had come to believe that the hieroglyphic images were actual gods when in reality they were only word-paintings. The Abbé Pluche received this doctrine from across the Channel and embellished it in his own inimitable scientific manner, but the heart of the matter was the same: There was one religion for the stupid Egyptians and another for those favored few initiated into the mysteries.

These eighteenth-century admirers and imitators of the ancients envisaged themselves as the legatees of secret truth, pantheist, Deist, or atheist, but like the wise men of old they were sworn to preserve this truth only for those prepared to receive it. While the philosophers were permitted absolute freedom for their speculations the multitude would have to be directed by the orthodox religious establishment. In part this ancient theory of the double truth was revived for the personal security of *philosophes,* but this was not the only motive: They really believed the common people to be incapable of behaving in a moral manner without the dread sanctions of religion. Among French Deists like Voltaire the idea persisted to the eve of the Revolution. Not until the Holbachians argued that the secular sovereign could dispense with the church as a prop of the social order did the double truth doctrine become superfluous in anticlerical thought. It was the hangman and not the priest who deterred the common people from committing crimes against property.

One branch of Deist thought, while it recognized the doctrine of the double truth as a historical reality in most ancient theocracies, was uneasy about this bifurcation of humanity. A great evil had been perpetrated by the purveyors of the twofold philosophy, perhaps the greatest iniquity of all time. The truth of natural religion and primitive monotheism had been shrouded from the mass of the people and preserved in secret not by benign philosophers but by wicked men in pursuit of power. Politicians or a priestly corps were endowed wtih intelligence and a shrewd scheming capacity, while the people were left in their ignorance and stupidity. Bishop Warburton out of a sense of solidarity with the priesthood of Egypt laid the original corruption of mankind to politicians—these later seduced the priests. Condorcet in the *Esquisse d'un tableau historique des progrès de l'esprit humain,* the classical expression of this theory after it had been usurped by the revolutionary atheists, imputed the initial plot to priests acting with complete self-consciousness. Variations on this theme are numerous: In Abbé Pluche's history the people fell into the error of idolatry naturally and the priests could do nothing to rescue them; in other versions the priests sinned by tolerating the frailty of the masses. Only a minority of theorists, Condorcet among them, carried the double truth doctrine to the point where the sacerdotal plotters, ensconced in their citadel of exclusive knowledge, became so lazy and routinized that they were themselves enveloped by the vapors of darkness they had originally generated.

Deists of a more tender persuasion denied wicked or evil intent on the part of the original founders of the mysteries; either their symbols were necessary forms of pictorial language used by ancient teachers in Oriental lands that had a natural addiction to imagistic figures, or they were a means of communication among all primitive humans not yet accustomed to rationalist modes of expression. Through error, that convenient eighteenth-century catchall, the meaning of the original primitive monotheist allegories had been forgotten, sometimes by the very priestly corps that had first devised them.

III

The ordinary Deist analysis of the degeneration of natural religion was often a monotonous reworking of a few classical themes. In the end it affirmed primitive monotheism as arbitrarily as did the orthodox dogma. In their psychopathology of religious experience, however, those Deist writers who recognized the insufficiency and essential poverty of the imposture theory introduced real novelty into eighteenth-century thought.

The study of psychology had been significantly stimulated by the seventeenth-century outbreaks of demonism and witch hunting. The trials were often long inquiries in which rational men brought up in the law participated and the judges showed a decent respect for testimony. Doctors were summoned to examine patients who were possessed by demons, and both ecclesiastical and secular authorities were on the lookout for pious frauds, the ras-

cally peasants who came to the church to be exorcised, with the
prospect of profit when they turned out to be the objects of a miraculous cure by the local priest. The weight of the empirical evidence was overwhelmingly in favor of the existence of demons. In
the seventeenth century a new scientific attitude had penetrated
even the study of demonology and it was possible to couple an
honest belief in demons with circumstantial detailed medical descriptions of the uniform characteristics of demoniacs, for it
seemed that even the devil had to obey the natural laws of his
profession. The words pathology and physiology crept into the
dissertations of faithful believers in the devil, in works like
Joannes Casparus Westphal's *Pathologia Daemoniaca, id est Ob-
servationes et Meditationes Physiologico-Magico-Medicae circa
Daemonomanias* (1707). It was equally scientific that the oppo-
nents of the devil, the good English Deists, should use the data assembled in works on the possessed as symptoms of plain insanity
and then extend their perceptions to all similar forms of religious
extravagance, pagan and Christian. In lieu of demons, a mechanistic psychology with great emphasis on the diverse effects of environmental conditions upon the senses was made to account for
most of the strange religious phenomena reported in antiquity, as
well as in the marvelous episodes of modern times.

Paradoxical as it may seem, the initiation of the study of individual and mass psychology was rooted not in any abstract scientific curiosity about the nature of man, but in a religious purpose
of great moment. English psychology was born the newest hand-
maiden of true religion. The Quaker illuminations and the Puritan fanaticism, the Anabaptist ravings and the convulsionaries,
the miracle-making Jansenists and the witchcraft accusations had
led the sober rational Deists to identify such manifestations a
priori with disease and madness. This was in one respect a polemical device, not unknown in our own contemporary intellectual
controversies, to explode millenarian visions by declaring them
projections of a sick body and a deranged mind, hence not wit-
nesses of God. Any religious experience other than the rational
perception of the coordinated workings of the mechanical uni-

verse under a Creator was for these Deists uniformly a symptom of disease like the ague or epilepsy. A "normal" or "natural" healthy psychic state was conceived as necessary not so much for worldly happiness as for a comprehension of the true God. Psychology was thus the consequence of a need for an objective criterion to evaluate aberrant religious experience, the differentiation between the true and the false prophet, an ancient problem that had once shaken the body politic of Israel. The modern enthusiast was false because he was in "distemper" and his knowledge of God was polluted. A German echo of this kind of thinking, in more pious garb, can be found later in the century in Johann Lorenz von Mosheim's *Philosophisch-theologische Abhandlung von den moralischen Krankheiten des menschlichen Geschlechts* (1771).

The two little-known English Deists John Trenchard and Thomas Gordon wrote at a crucial intermediary moment in the development of the psychology of religion. They came in the wake of the pioneer revolutionary Dutch and French works, the exposures of the Greco-Roman and Hebrew religious artifices and superstitions by Van Dale and Fontenelle, Balthasar Bekker's exile of devils from the world and their enchainment in hell, a stream of medical investigations of demoniacs, and above all Bayle's eclectic assimilation both of priestly imposture and psychopathological behavior as plausible explanations for the strange manifestations of credulity ancient and modern. Trenchard and Gordon were steeped in other English analyses of religious enthusiasm, in Burton's famous *Anatomy of Melancholy* and in Shaftesbury's essays. At times their works, which have a journalistic character, were virtual paraphrases of more eminent predecessors, but no other writings of the period were as candid in their factual description of religious experience and as forceful in their free and easy use of a vigorous English diction reminiscent of the polemics of the Revolution, or as acute in their diagnosis of the psychic origins of religious mysticism.

Trenchard's *Natural History of Superstition*—the scientific title is noteworthy—dated 1709, has never been reprinted and is a great rarity. When Trenchard collaborated with Thomas Gordon in the publication of the *Independent Whig* in 1720, his old arguments were presented in an even more vehement style and amplified with new themes. This series of essays on politics and religion, which lived up to its title, was an extraordinary success, saw many re-editions, and even made its way across the Atlantic. Though it is not cited in his writings, David Hume probably perused it; at least many of his observations on the psychology of religion parallel its reasoning. The Bishop of Man condemned this "most pestilent book" in a bull, despite the honest Deism of its authors and their adoration of Christ. If the original text was no more sacrilegious than the run of Deist literature of the Tindal variety, its later fortunes on the Continent seem to justify the bishop's censure, for it was translated by the atheist Holbach and appropriated by the "great Synagogue." The wicked baron also pretended that *La Contagion sacrée* was a translation of *The Natural History of Superstition,* but it was really introduced only in one or two sections and should not bear the onus for the whole of Holbach's outright blasphemy.[6]

Religious ideas like those which Conyers Middleton, the respectable librarian of Trinity College, paraded publicly in the first decades of the eighteenth century would have been considered terrible heresies in France. In its very first number on January 20, 1720, the *Independent Whig* highlighted the differences in the temper of the two societies, rejoicing in English spiritual liberty. True there were freethinking abbés in Paris, but they did not hold the public position of a Tillotson. Bishop Warburton, in England a "bigot" who used his ecclesiastical powers to intimidate libertines, was on the Continent a *philosophe* whose early writings were widely admired. But as the century wore on, English treatises on theological subjects tended to become more conservative, stereotyped, and orthodox. The wild days of Toland and Collins were soon over, and Hume avoided publication of his famous dialogue during his lifetime. In France in the meantime the radical temper had possessed society. With the triumph of the philosophical sect in the 1760s, all manner of flagrant violations of moderate opinion were perpetrated, not with the royal patent, to be sure, but nevertheless with general knowledge and amid widespread literary comment. It was during this period that the robust early-eighteenth-century English Deists, pretty much passé in their own country, were introduced into France, where they served no longer the cause of the pure love of a benign God and a gentle Jesus, but the most outrageous atheism, which mocked Adam, Abraham, Christ, and the pagan gods in the same licentious tone.

The *Independent Whig* and the little essay on superstition that preceded it were still written in the earthy language of seventeenth-century Puritan sermons, though their subject was the contempt of hellfire. The ideas were far less elegantly expressed than in their later version in Hume, who wrote with Cicero, Horace, and Lucretius peering over his shoulder and guiding his hand. The journalism of Trenchard and Gordon was rough, and even Holbach thinned out many passages of the original text to conform to the taste of his genteel French atheists. The early-eighteenth-century English Deists wrote the way Diderot often talked. "Sometimes you are to scarify your Backside for the Healing of your Soul," sneered the *Independent Whig* on October 5, 1720, "and reconcile yourself to Heaven by the Dint of Lashings which will sometimes serve for another *Purpose;* and so a Scourge made of Broom, is made the Scourge of God." Trenchard and Gordon were fighting popery, priests, their English imitators in the Anglican Church, enthusiastic Protestant sectarians of every variety. Theirs was not a mild gentlemanly unitarianism. It was Deism militant, a ferocious, rampant, sarcastic, battling, idol-breaking, priest-hating, fanatic-loathing crusade. But it was far from devoid of analytic elements; the rhetoric always contained a hard rationalist kernel.

For these Deists religious experience was plainly divisible into two categories, the true and the false. A belief in a rational Creator and in the gospel of Christ preaching love was the totality of the true religion, even more abbreviated than Herbert of Cherbury's. All other religious manifestations were false, and these were the subject of Trenchard's first inquiry in 1709 into the origins and etiology of superstition, not a minor concern since it comprised the cult practices and creeds of most human beings throughout all time. Half a century before the publication of Hume's magisterial essay, *The Natural History of Superstition* posed fundamental questions related to the psychology of religious emotion. Why were men who were possessed by "panick fears" prone to superstition? Why did they have bizarre religious feelings and perform unnatural acts in the name of God? How could rational men be so readily deceived by priestly frauds? How was it possible for them to believe in myths of abominable gods as if they were realities? How could a religious mystic credit his hallucinations? For answers Trenchard turned to a study of human nature, "to examine into the frame and constitution of our own Bodies, and search into the causes of our Passions and Infirmities."[7] There he discovered why the mind, for all its perfection, had been misled and betrayed into superstition, why despite the wondrous natural order of the world and the excellence of the human mechanism it had been possible for priests to perpetrate sacerdotal deceits and for enthusiasts to see visions.

Trenchard first offered a secular physiological equivalent of original sin. There was in fact "something innate in our Constitutions" which made us susceptible to these delusions. Man, governed by the postulates of Lockian sensationalism, sought to avoid pain, or what he imagined might hurt him. Above all, he was preoccupied with that greatest pain, death, and what transpired in the hereafter. Since man was both inquisitive and a cause-seeker, as Fontenelle had already defined him, he was driven by a passionate desire to know the identity and intentions of his potential pain-inflicter; but unfortunately the cause of things was hidden, and in his anxious bewilderment he accepted either the word of authority or whatever his imagination concocted at random. This same theme can be discovered in a crude form in John Toland and later, expressed with subtlety, in Nicolas Fréret's *Lettre de Thrasybule à Leucippe*, which the Baron d'Holbach published.[8] The prospect of death had led men to the invention of the pagan gods and the myriad arts of divination, which Trenchard catalogued in a Joyce-like passage clearly lifted from Balthasar Bekker, *De Beto-verde Weereld:*

To these Weaknesses and our own, and Frauds of others, we owe the Heathen Gods and Goddesses, Oracles and Prophets, Nimphs and Satyrs, Fawns and Tritons, Furies and Demons, most of the Stories of Conjurers and Witches, Spirits and Apparitions, Fairies and Hobgoblins, the Doctrine of Prognosticks, the numerous ways of Divination, viz. Oniromancy, Sideromancy, Tephranomancy, Botonomancy, Crommyomancy, Cleromancy, Aeromancy, Onomatomancy, Arithomancy, Geomancy, Alectryomancy, Cephalomancy, Axinomancy, Coscinomancy, Hydromancy, Onychomancy, Dactylomancy, Christallomancy, Cataptromancy, Gastromancy, Lecanomancy, Alphitomancy, Chiromancy, Orneomancy, and Necromancy, Horoscopy, Astrology and Augury, Metoposcopy and Palmistry, the fear of Eclipse, Comets, Meteors, Earthquakes, Inundations, and any uncommon Appearances, though never so much depending upon Natural and Necessary Causes, nor are there wanting People otherwise of good understanding, who are affected with the falling of a Salt-Seller, crossing of a Hare, croaking of a Raven, howling of Dogs, screaching of Owls, the motion of Worms in a Bedsteed, mistaken for Death-Watches, and other senseless and trifling accidents.[9]

During the ceremonials of divination the clients actually saw visions that appeased their hunger for a knowledge of their fate, and they really believed that they had visited heaven and hell. Trenchard took directly out of Pierre Bayle a hypothesis explaining the psychophysiological operations of the delusion. Under given circumstances, often artificially arranged, inner stimuli in the body aroused visions, which were not contradicted by the senses that normally recorded impressions from the outside. The key to hallucinations was thus the blockage of communication with the real world, "when the Organs of Sense (which are the Avenues and Doors to let in external objects) are shut and locked up."[10] Loss of contact occurred under a wide variety of circumstances: during sleep, in states of delirium, in madness, in ordinary physical sickness, in melancholy, in states of exclusive concentration on single objects, under the shock of environmental conditions that terrified or deceived. These situations all had in common the fact that the internally generated images "reign without any Rival" and are continually "striking strongly upon, and affecting the Brain, Spirits, or Organ where the imaginative faculty resides."[11] This adaptation of Lockian epistemology adequately explained the "inward light" of the visionaries cut off from the outward senses, the only "conduits of knowledge." Any hallucination was then believed as reality. The victims "embrace their own Clouds and Foggs for Deities"; some may see "beatifick visions," others "Divels with instruments of Fear and Horrour." Melancholy and "hypocondriack men" might have specific delusions, like the Reverend Mr. Peling who believed himself pregnant. A man might think he was a glass, a bottle, a god, the Messiah, the pope, a dog, cat, or wolf. He might imagine, as did John Beaumont, author of *An Historical, Physiological and Theological Treatise of Spirits, Apparitions, Witchcrafts and other Magical Practices . . . With a Refutation of Dr. Bekker's World Bewitch'd; and other Authors that have opposed the Belief of them* (1705), that he had conversations with spirits, and record them. "Many instances of this kind are to be found in Burton's Melancholy, and more to be seen in Bedlam."[12]

Trenchard was well acquainted with the contemporary literature of psychopathological experience; his innovation was to identify these delusions with any nonrationalist religious perception and to assign to them all a uniform physiological cause. Monastic spiritual exercises and their physical accompaniments such as fasting, whipping, and seclusion were merely mechanical devices that induced psychic states akin to those generated by bodily illness and ordinary mental derangement. True religion exhilarated the spirit, but those monks who enjoyed reputations for exceptional piety had invariably been melancholic recluses. These men were sick, for it was unnatural to sequester oneself. Their physical organs were disturbed and consequently their visions both waking and asleep, far from being revelations of true religion, were nothing but the symptoms of disease.

Trenchard's conception of the interrelations between body and soul, while derivative from seventeenth-century psychology and well known to Spinoza, was set forth in terms that would have been completely comprehensible toward the end of the century to Dr. Cabanis the *idéologue,* reflecting on the reciprocal influences of the physical and the spiritual (with the substitution of *la nature* for Divine Wisdom, of course): "It's evident the Divine Wisdom hath so formed and united our Souls and Bodies that they mutually act upon one another, insomuch that there is no action of the Mind that does not cause a correspondent one in the Body; nor no motion of the Body that does not produce a suitable affection in the Mind."[13] In this Deist rehabilitation of the flesh the body, no longer conceived of as the evil tyrant of the mind, had a parallel being, and its elementary requirements could not be denied without immediate deleterious morbid reactions in the spirit. When a monk castigated the flesh he generated spiritual illness, insanity.

For Trenchard, the phantasms of the religionist were not merely the concern of a lone fanatic, for such hallucinations were readily communicable to great masses of people. In literary images that were an admixture of Epicurean and Newtonian physics—not as preposterous a combination as one might imagine—adapted to human bodies, Trenchard devised a physical theory to account for the rapid spread of religious mania. "Both Mind and Body are visibly affected with the actions of other beings, and of one another, and wherever we move we are surrounded with Bodies, all of which in some degree operate upon us. . . . Besides everything in Nature is in constant Motion, and perpetually emitting Effluviums and minute Particles of its Substance, which operate upon, and strike other Bodies."[14] Effluvia rather than witchcraft might naturalistically account for the convulsive fits of children in the proximity of old hags. "And the poisonous and melancholy Vapours streaming from an Enthusiast, cause distraction and Raving as well as the Bite of a Mad Dog." In an effort to explain the spread of religious enthusiasm and sympathies Trenchard tried musical analogies. "When two violins are tuned alike if you strike upon one, the other sounds."[15] George Keith in his famous exposure, *The Magick of Quakerism* (1707), had studied the sensitivity that the brethren had perfected in recognizing each other's effluvia, and many of Trenchard's reflections are based on his analysis of their experience.

Lord Shaftesbury was simultaneously teaching the same doctrine as Trenchard. In the *Soliloquy: or Advice to an Author*, first printed in 1710 and in 1711 incorporated in the *Characteristicks of Men, Manners, Opinions, Times*, he raised psychology to an eminence above all other science and knowledge, because its norms were determinant in distinguishing between true and false religion. The "study of human affection . . . has not its name, as other philosophies, from the mere subtlety and nicety of the speculation, but by way of excellence, from its being superior to all other speculations, from its presiding over all other sciences and occupations, teaching the measure of each, and assigning the just value of everything in life. By this science religion itself is judged, spirits are searched, prophecies proved, miracles distinguished: the sole measure and standard being taken from moral rectitude, and from the discernment of what is sound and just in the affections."[16] This aristocratic, introspective invalid psychologized all religious emotion in the *Characteristicks*, one of the most influential treatises of the age. Shaftesbury, who was Bayle's friend during his long stay in Holland, had no doubt discussed psychopathic religious experiences with him, but the problem of influence should not be resolved mehanically; Bayle wrote few passages that equal Shaftesbury's abnormal psychology of religion. A Whig in politics, like Trenchard and Gordon, he ridiculed the religious enthusiasts of all nations, Jews, Greeks, Catholics, Puritans, French Protestants. In passages of superb acumen he described the fanatic who was profoundly convinced of the divine source of his inspiration, the prophetic seer, the wild-eyed possessed one, transformed in an instant into the bigot, the persecutor, the inquisitor. Many of the clumsily phrased psychological reflections of La Mettrie and Holbach on the relationship between fanaticism and cruelty were anticipated in these elegant lordly essays written in a classical style that still betrays the schoolboy who could converse in the Latin of Horace.

Men had projected their own foul moods into their gods. A religion born of fear and excitation was impure because it derived from a psychological malaise, was the thesis of the *Letter concerning Enthusiasm* (1708), also reprinted in the *Characteristicks*. "We can never be fit to contemplate anything above us, when we are in no condition to look into ourselves, and calmly examine the temper of our own mind and passions. For then it is we see wrath, and fury, and revenge, and terrors in the Deity; when we are full of disturbances and fears within, and have, by sufferance and anxiety, lost so much of the natural calm and easiness of our temper."[17] The embittered dissenter created a vicious and jealous God; men in good humor would never attribute vengefulness and terrible punishments to Him. Nature bore men no malice and they should not impute to the Deity the defects, imperfections, and passions that existed only in themselves. Benign Deists like Shaftesbury, for whom true Christianity was a religion of humanity, tried to establish sordid psychological origins for the terrible Christian prophecies of universal destruction and of awful retribution on sinners in the next world. Such ravings sprang from sour natures and were incompatible with the image of a God of love. The religious enthusiast had to be cured—and either wit or mockery were the remedies, never persecution. But why these outbursts of "distemper"? Shaftesbury's reply was an analogy naïvely physiological. "There are certain humours in mankind which of necessity must have vent. The human mind and body are both of them naturally subject to commotions: and as there are strange ferments in the blood, which in many bodies occasion of extraordinary discharge; so in reason, too, there are heterogeneous particles which must be thrown off by fermentation."[18]

The descriptions of mass delusions and popular religious mania in the *Letter concerning Enthusiasm* were in the same spirit as *The Natural History of Superstition*. The idea of a sacred contagion was adorned with the Lucretian "scientificisms" in which Trenchard delighted.

And in this state their very looks are infectious. The fury flies from face
to face; and the disease is no sooner seen than caught. They who in a
better situation of mind have beheld a multitude under the power of
this passion, have owned that they saw in the countenances of men something more ghastly and terrible than at other times is expressed on the
most passionate occasion. . . . And thus is religion also panic; when
enthusiasm of any kind gets up, as oft, on melancholy occasions, it will
do. For vapors naturally rise; and in bad times especially, when the
spirits of men are low, as either in public calamities, or during the un-
wholesomeness of air or diet, or when convulsions happen in nature,
storms, earthquakes, or other amazing prodigies.[19]

After the *Independent Whig* submitted organized religious institutions, ancient and modern, to rational analysis, it discovered
that the same techniques of deceit had been practiced in all ages.
There had always been dupes, ordinary people subject to a variety
of passions, which in their ignorance and state of emotional ex-
citability they attributed to supernatural powers; and above them
had hovered the canny impostors, men who had made shrewd observations on the psychological infirmities of mankind in order to
exploit them. "There is not a living Creature in the Universe,
which has not some innate Weakness, or original Imbecility coeval
to its Being: that is, some Inclinations or Disgusts, some peculiar
Desires or Fears which render it easy Prey to other animals, who,
from their constitutional Sagacity or Experience, know how to
take Advange of this Infirmity. . . . The peculiar Foible of Mankind, is Superstition, or an intrinsick and pannick Fear of invisible and unknown Beings."[20] Knowledge of the "sympathetic
emotions" and the spontaneous human reactions of wonderment
had historically been the major psychic weapon in the arsenal of
imposture. The wily ones had learned how these feelings could be
artificially stimulated in others, they had discovered the "secret of
hitting luckily upon this Foible and native imbecility of Mankind," and once possessed of this power they could manipulate the
dupes as they pleased.

Since pathological religious phenomena were diseases, they
were virtually the same in modern times as in antiquity. The
Quakers were like an "Infamous Sect in Old Rome," the Pythian

prophetess, the sibyls, the *Alumbrados* in Spain. In one passage of the *Natural History*, patently Burtonian, Trenchard had identified the enthusiast as a psychological type naturally prone to the disease, and he gave him a name, the *Atra-bilis* or melancholy man characterized by "Inquietude and Alienation of the Mind, Grief, Anxiety, Dejection, Absurd Thoughts, Anxious and Pannick Fears, and a desire for Solitude."[21] In another he likened religious enthusiasm to inebriation. His dramatic description of the violent aggressiveness and maniacal destructiveness of this melancholy, self-tortured, diseased fanatic should be familiar to modern psychologists. "Aversion, Pride and Fury in the shape of Zeal, like a mighty Storm ruffles his Mind into Beating Billows, and Boisterous Fluctuations: At last he is all in a Rage, and no Church Buckets to quench his Fiery Religion, Religion and the Glory of God drives him on: The Holy Enthusiastick longs to Feast and Riot upon humane Sacrifices, turn Cities and Nations into Shambles, and destroy with Fire and Sword such who dare thwart his Frenzy and all the while like another Nero, Plays upon his Harpe, and sings Te Deum at the Conflagration."[22]

The Deist psychopathology of enthusiasm was revived in the inquiry into the nature of primitive mentality and the genesis of religion later in the century. While the Deists themselves remained steadfast in their doctrine of original monotheism, their empirical analysis of existing religious fanaticism, a degeneration of truth into a "rout of ceremonies," was adapted to another historical context once the rationalist evolutionary idea of progress was formulated. In defining the emotional situation of the primitive worshipers of cruel, savage gods, eighteenth-century atheists, above all Holbachians, merely transposed to aboriginal man the ugly characteristics of the contemporary fanatic personality that Shaftesbury and Trenchard had anatomized. "Pannick fear," which the Deist doctors of souls had diagnosed clinically among their possessed fellows, was assimilated to the ancient fear-theory of the origins of religion. The terror-stricken savage and the pagan of antiquity who spawned religions were both psychically ill. They were victims of *la contagion sacrée*.

3 A PSYCHOLOGY OF
EVERYDAY RELIGION

I N 1757 appeared the classical eighteenth-century document on
the psychology of religion, David Hume's essay *The Natural
History of Religion*. The text was preceded by a brief "Author's
Introduction," prompted largely by fear of the formidable Bishop
William Warburton, who threatened to enlist the attorney-general
on the side of the gods. It should be read with the intonations of
Hume's ambiguous intent, rather than in the bland manner in
which it was assimilated by the innocent:

As every enquiry, which regards religion, is of the utmost importance,
there are two questions in particular, which challenge our attention, to
wit, that concerning its foundation in reason, and that concerning its origin in human nature. Happily, the first question, which is the most
important, admits of the most obvious, at least, the clearest, solution.
The whole frame of nature bespeaks an intelligent author; and no rational enquirer can, after serious reflection, suspend his belief a moment
with regard to the primary principles of genuine Theism and Religion.
But the other question, concerning the origin of religion in human nature, is exposed to some more difficulty.[1]

In making this distinction Hume tries to bypass the philosophy
of religion as formulated by major thinkers of the seventeenth and
eighteenth centuries. He would not be dealing with Spinoza's
God, or Herbert of Cherbury's God, or Voltaire's God; nor would
he be wrestling with the problem of the existence of God as it was
treated in his own *Dialogues concerning Natural Religion*, whose

publication he suppressed, or in such militant atheistic refutations of a divinity as would later be propounded by the Baron d'Holbach and the Marquis de Sade. Following his lead one can address oneself to the second of Hume's questions, the origin of religion in human nature.

I

How did European writers in the eighteenth century explain the varieties of religious behavior in the orthodox establishments, Catholic, Protestant, and Jewish, with which they had immediate direct experience? What did they make of the behavior of contemporary heathens in the worlds of savage and civilized paganism, knowledge of whose ceremonies had penetrated their consciousness through the reports in an ever-swelling volume of travel literature? The investigation of religious practice—recognized to be a virtually universal human phenomenon, despite a few isolated accounts of religionless savage peoples—led to the invention of a full-fledged psychology of religion, an explanation of mass behavior, distinct from the question of the truth or falsity of one or another belief. The documentation was vast: Source materials could be collected from the literature of classical antiquity, from the Church Fathers, from the long parade of Christian heresies and sects, and could be juxtaposed with descriptions in heavy multi-tomed compendia of religious ceremonials current in all parts of the world. These illustrated works were very much in vogue, testimony to the widespread curiosity about every conceivable form of alien religion. Without the historicist preconceptions that later burdened the nineteenth century, the analysts of the eighteenth could breezily make comparisons, fix parallels, establish identities among specimens from all ages and places as if they were dealing with flora and fauna. The anticlerical motives of many of the authors are patent: Their psychology of religion was hardly a dispassionate science, and often diagnoses of fetish cults in Guinea (*vide* Charles de Brosses, *Du culte des dieux fétiches*), or Ngombos in the Congo (*vide* Baron d'Holbach), or the deceiving mechanisms of ancient Greek priests (*vide* Fontenelle) were really aimed at rituals closer to home. Even if these studies

were tainted by their underlying purpose, their method had at
least the trappings of science. Evidence was assembled, hypotheses
were framed, as, for example Vico's and Hume's constructs of the
emotions of primitive savages, and conclusions were reached. The
Dutch scholar Antonius Van Dale meticulously examined the Old
and New Testaments and rabbinic literature for the footprints of
idolatry; Balthasar Bekker probed the travel literature of the
nations for devil-worshipers. They were drawing up *catalogues
raisonnés* of esoteric rites even as Presbyterian divines in mid-
seventeenth-century England had compiled lengthy catalogues of
heresies and sectarian deviations.

There is no eighteenth-century book specifically entitled "The
Psychology of Religion," though the neologism "psychology" had
been around since Goclenius, a German professor, invented the
term in the sixteenth century. Reflections on the subject, however,
were strewn about in many different types of writing—natural histories of superstition, natural histories of religion, anatomies of
religious melancholy and enthusiasm. Licentious novels—of
which Diderot's *La Religieuse* was the most notorious—depicted
the psychological devastation wrought by religion on the inmates
of monasteries and convents. Essays and books on education analyzed the psychic injuries inflicted on the young by prevailing
popular religions. *Le Christianisme dévoilé* and *La Contagion
sacrée* were characteristic titles from the Baron d'Holbach's atheist
laboratory, which treated all religion as pathological. But,
strangely enough, by the end of the century many of the ideas
first developed by the antagonists of religion found their way into
Christian apologetics. The emotive character of religion, once de-
cried as a weakness, was abruptly turned into a primary virtue by
the Germans Hamann and Herder.

In the eighteenth century most firsthand observers of other
people's religious behavior took a completely external view. They
merely described ceremonial religious conduct and penetrated no
further; at best they left laconic reports of the actors' general intent in engaging in certain performances. The explorers and
priests who watched savage rites in various parts of the world

tended to restrict themselves to silent pictures with a few stock captions such as "Hindus mourning the dead." Homebodies in Paris and London then tried to infuse these lifeless descriptions with meaning and became psychologists of religion after a fashion. True believers of course were for the most part untouched by this literature; they were satisfied that their own religion and its ceremonials had been revealed to their ancestors in the past, and it was their duty to continue to believe and worship and obey commandments that could not be questioned. On occasion a particular ceremonial might be "explained" as a commemorative or symbolic act, but this did not constitute a psychological interpretation. Yet even the most orthodox, when confronted with aberrant religious behavior in their midst, were drawn into the widely cast net of the eighteenth-century psychology of religion.

Some risks were run by eighteenth-century thinkers inquiring directly into the origins of Judaism and Christianity or religion *tout court*. But since the most learned religious geographers of the seventeenth century, such as the antiquarian and astronomer Edward Brerewood, had estimated that at least five-sixths of the globe was inhabited by pagans and infidels, an extensive field of investigation was open even to orthodox thinkers. Disbelievers, needless to add, gladly availed themselves of the cover of studies of the nature of paganism, ancient and modern. Moreover, within the Christian lands of Europe there were a number of types of religious behavior which, since the Renaissance and the Reformation, could be diagnosed clinically without incurring official censure from the orthodox. For example, in Protestant countries the saint-worship and monasticism of Catholic countries could be identified with pagan rituals from antiquity and the behavior of contemporary American savages, and could then be discussed as pathological or diabolical phenomena. Among both Protestants and Catholics, fanatical "enthusiasm" and mystical pretensions, always regarded uneasily in orthodox establishments, could be treated as religious pathology that required the understanding of physicians as well as clergymen. Granted that such behavior was inspired by demons, from the Renaissance on it was legitimate to search into the mechanics that they used in gaining possession of their victims. This, too, opened the door to naturalistic analyses, especially in connection with the trial of witches.

Eighteenth-century thinkers, who treated the critical study of popular religion among the ancients with the respect due to ancestors, had inherited a body of basic conceptions and theories. Lucretius and Lucian were favorites of the age. Moralists like Cicero had already distinguished between a philosophical belief in the gods and popular religion, and had analyzed both. But the Church Fathers were perhaps the richest source books for the analysis of pagan behavior. Voltaire was deeply immersed in patristic literature, as is evident from even a cursory examination of his books and their marginalia; and the Church Fathers, in fighting the abominable rites of pagans, Gnostics, and heretics, had left lurid commentaries on religious practices that could be adapted to serve the purposes of eighteenth-century anticlerical unveilers of the secret springs of all religion. Euhemeristic explanations of the pagan gods as mere kings who had divinized themselves—a favorite form of interpretation among the learned in the seventeenth and eighteenth centuries, for whom it provided much academic employment—had, after all, been transmitted to modern times primarily through the polemics of the Church Fathers against the reality of the pagan gods.

Timeworn religious problems within monotheistic religions, as well as the unmasking of paganism in antiquity, nourished eighteenth-century writers with ideas on the psychological nature of religion itself. The *philosophes* were not averse to learning from their orthodox enemies. One of the oldest concerns of Judaism and Christianity was how to distinguish between true and false prophecy. The medieval Jewish philosopher Maimonides had devoted large parts of a number of treatises to tests for discovering a false prophet. By the seventeenth century, his reasoning had been absorbed into the Christian world, and especially in England and Holland there grew up a voluminous literature that concentrated on the signs whereby fanatical pretenders to direct communication with God could be detected. Burton's *Anatomy of*

Melancholy of 1621 includes a large section on religious melancholy, by which he meant religious manias in all times and places; his express intention was to differentiate true religion from superstitious and pathological behavior. When materials from his treatise were picked up by the two early-eighteenth-century Whig pamphleteers John Trenchard and Thomas Gordon, they initiated a line of thought that was ultimately diverted to a wholly different end. Trenchard's *Natural History of Superstition* was reflected in Hume's *Natural History of Religion* in the middle of the century, and finally in Holbach's *La Contagion sacrée, ou histoire naturelle de la superstition* (1768), an exposition of outright atheism and a unique psychology of religion. Thus an orthodox religious preoccupation, the differentiation of true from false prophecy, could eventuate, after a number of intellectual zigzags, in an analysis of *all* religion as a disease.

Eighteenth-century writers, when they examined popular religious behavior, were hardly ploughing virgin soil. To be sure, they knew the classical studies bettter than the works of Renaissance and Reformation doctors like Girolamo Cardano and Johann Wier and Peter van Foreest. As was the manner of the age, they often reiterated old ideas as if they were totally new discoveries, or put forth in greater detail propositions for which one can find hints and origins in previous literature. But they also introduced fresh conceptions. The polemical purpose of their work lent passion to their writing, and the arguments of their predecessors infiltrated European thought of later ages in the form that the *philosophes* gave them.

Without presuming to dwell on all aspects of the eighteenth-century psychology of religion, I shall try to illuminate a few of its basic principles. It should be taken for granted that in seeking the common denominators among a group of writers, I make no pretense to a comprehensive evaluation of any individual thinker's views. The sworn philosophical enemies of the *esprit de système* left no coordinated body of reflections on the subject that preoccupied them perhaps more than any other: How could man, capable of reason, descend to the childishness, cruelty, and mad-

ness of most religious practices? A formal presentation may bestow
more of a structure on their thought than they would have accepted; and while hypostatizing an eighteenth-century body of
radical thought on the psychology of religion one has to be aware
of the great diversity of opinion among Enlightenment writers
and the frequent contradictions within them. We are dealing with
philosophes, not philosophers.

Perhaps the most striking example of the *philosophes'* psycholo-
gizing of popular belief is their manipulation of the relation between fear and belief in God. The rabbis' Fear of God—the Yirat
Ha-shem, Fear of the Name—was traditionally one of the loftiest
attributes of the religious man. For some Reformation theologians, *Gottesfurcht* became the pivot of religious belief. Among
the *philosophes,* fear of God was transformed into a negative trait
of the religious personality, the source of much that was stupid,
cruel, and self-destructive in religious behavior. Popular religion,
with its major premise that God had a special concern for the
particular of each individual, was for most *philosophes* the offspring of man's anxiety, which took the form of exaggerating fears
of the future as well as hopes for the future. On balance, fear pre-
dominated over hope in the emotional equipment of men (hope
was always accompanied by the anxious fear that it might not be
fulfilled), and the ancient Lucretian dictum that in the beginning
the gods were born of fear was reaffirmed.

The eighteenth century added novel elements to this underlying psychological theory. Since the experience of fear was not
isolated but tended to involve and draw along with it other emotions, fear gave rise to a whole complex of undesirable behavior
patterns. It brought men to such a state of anxiety that they lost
their rational faculties and jumped at any prospect or promise of
removing the cause of fear or mitigating the punishment and pain
they dreaded. They fell into a mire of superstitions, behaving toward gods as they would toward powerful, malevolent men they
encountered. The Baron d'Holbach invented the neologism *an-
thropomorphism* to describe the projection of human emotion
into the gods, before whom men cringed as if they were angry,

exigent, outsized human beings. Fear-stricken believers turned over money and goods and choice objects to fakir priests who offered them alleviation of pain in this world and the promise of reduction of pain in the next. "In all ages," Voltaire wrote, "men have believed that they could appease the gods by offerings, because one often calms the rage of men by giving them gifts, and because we have always made God in our image. . . . It is quite simple reasoning to offer our gods what is most precious to us. And it is even more natural that the priests should demand such sacrifices, since they have always divided everything with Heaven and theirs is the best portion."[2]

Sometimes fear was so great that men sacrificed their children and inflicted punishment on themselves, in monstrous violation of the natural pleasure principle, in order to forestall some greater punishment threatened by the raging, unseen gods. Men had to give conspicuous proof of denying themselves pleasure and they tormented themselves spiritually and physically until they reached the point of madness. So limitless was their fear of the infinite God they had invented that they even sacrificed a god to appease his fury, an Holbachian conceit that Nietzsche in his deliberately scandalous interpretation of Christ later adopted without benefit of citation.

Fear and self-denial created a sour temper, a mean disposition, which in turn induced aggressive and cruel conduct. The sufferer has a natural tendency to make others suffer. In monotheism the power of one God was maximized—as contrasted with the division of spheres of influence among the myriad gods of polytheism—and fear of Him was so consuming that the monotheist believer tended to be the most timorous of creatures and the most cruel to enemies of the religion upon which he was fixated. David Hartley's doctrine of association, expounded in the *Observations on Man* (1749), an idea common enough in various guises in eighteenth-century thought, made this constant overflow of the emotion of fear into all aspects of existence quite plausible. Emotions set off sympathetic vibrations like musical instruments, Hume taught.

Such thinking carried *philosophes* to the deduction that there were parallel gradations in the scales of natural fearsomeness and superstitious behavior. Those persons who were weakest either by nature or as a consequence of their situation in the world were, experience showed, the most frightened and superstition-ridden. Travel literature as Hume read it revealed to him the spectacle of a savage terrified because the manifest uncertainties of nature made his existence miserable and precarious, subject to sudden, violent cataclysms before which he was helpless. Vico's primitives, overwhelmed by the shock of thunder and lightning after the post-diluvian drying out of the earth, never recovered from their initial terror. Sailors whose condition placed them in constant dread of drowning were naturally more superstitious than other men. Women and children and the aged, who suffered from grossly exaggerated fears because of their unprotected state, were given to morbid and abject beliefs about the supernatural.

Men were so prone to forge into absolute bonds chance coincidences of association that if the sight of an insect, beast, or plant accompanied misfortune they would ever afterward be afraid of it, and in order to placate it would soon come to worship the thing irrespective of how vile it might be. This observation helped men as widely separated in temperament as the Président de Brosses and the Baron d'Holbach to account for the fetishism of Africa and the Egyptian adoration of animals, so baffling to an Enlightenment thinker. Weak-minded savages, who could not reason, fell easy victim to such associations; and even ordinary people in civilized countries made connections of this character. The nature of the response depended on a man's emotional state, the *philosophes* had learned from Spinoza, their secret master. In health and good spirits, a man paid no attention to counsel, he had reflected in the *Tractatus Theologico-Politicus;* in the dire straits of misfortune, he flung himself upon the first bystander and begged for advice. Similarly, sickness and the catastrophes that struck all men, primitive and civilized, ignorant and learned, made them turn to gods for succor.

A corollary of the fear theory bred a small measure of hopefulness for an enlightened mankind of the future even among skeptical philosophers like Hume. In a state of civility where fears were somewhat diminished because of the relative security of urban living—oh, *tempora mutantur!*—men became a bit less timorous, hence less superstitious, that is, less prone to believe in false causes and effects, and therefore, to follow out the chain of rational consequences, less fanatical in their religion. But Hume had little faith that the mass of mankind, and even the philosophers most of the time, would ever be free from the anxieties inspired by the fear of death; hence the end of superstition and superstitious religion was not to be expected. The outright atheist Holbach was sometimes more sanguine. Through the progress of the human mind—and he used the phrase "les progrès de l'esprit humain" as early as 1758—it could be proved to men that there were no gods. Under atheism fear of the gods and all its noxious consequences would be banished and men would be naturally happier.

But other members of the Holbach circle, like the young engineer Nicolas Boulanger, were not quite as confident of the future as Holbach himself. For Boulanger writing *L'Antiquité dévoilée,* the fears and sadness expressed in the myths and ceremonies of all religions were the natural reactions of the survivors of deluges that periodically inundated the earth. All religions were for him repetitive transmissions of accounts of a deluge and they were uniformly lugubrious, the litanies of victims who were traumatized, psychologically driven to repeat over and over again the tale of their suffering in poetic and symbolic forms, even as you and I never weary of recounting the tale of some misfortune. Since periodic catastrophes were inevitable, this religion of fear and mourning would be constantly renewed, though in the enlightened stages of a civilization's cycle, in the interim before the next deluge, knowledge of the true origin of religious emotion might temporarily liberate men from *total* enthrallment to its superstitions.

The overwhelming number of *philosophes* who rooted the popular religions in fear judged them destructive of human happiness (Vico was the exception). Diderot was perhaps the most persuasive of the psychologists of fear-religion when he dwelt on its distortion of human personality. In an extravagant excursion in one of his

Salons he wickedly raised the possibility of another religion alternative to Christianity with its apotheosis of fear and suffering, what Holbach called the religion of a *dieu pauvre et crucifié*. Diderot maliciously suggested that if Western culture had inherited a Christ who had an affair with the Magdalene and at a joyous wedding banquet in Cana, between two wines, "caressed the breasts of one of the bridesmaids and the buttocks of Saint John," a spirit of delight would have spread throughout all the adherents of this sensuous religion. In its stead Europeans had inherited the sufferings of the Man of Sorrows.[3]

In a few passages the Baron d'Holbach in his lumbering way tried to look behind the fear syndrome of man that made him fabricate gods and to ask forthrightly why the creature was so frightened. The run of *philosophes* operated on the premise that terror of death was the ultimate emotion and required no further explanation. Holbach ventured to suggest that the ubiquity of this fear, which engendered a belief in a deity, demanded deeper probing. Man feared because as an infant he was naturally necessitous, and from the first moment of his existence there were others about who could satisfy the needs he made known through cries of pain. This reliance upon "the others who were stronger," usually his parents, became deeply ingrained in his nature, and when he grew to adulthood the dependence upon an almighty god to satisfy his needs and allay his suffering was fortified by the "remembrance" (the word is Holbach's) of his infantile state of utter helplessness. The Freud of the *Future of an Illusion* would have appreciated this analysis.

In many areas the radical materialist *philosophes* introduced a time-dimension into their psychological systems—the perseveration of first memories of childhood, the fixation upon the early catastrophes of the race that then became embedded in myths and religious rites, the power of error transmitted from primitive times through habit and custom. The Holbachian *philosophes* had faith that enlightenment could break the historical bonds that fettered mankind to the superstitions of its forefathers, or at least might weaken them.

The nature of the fear syndrome, when further explored, had led to an explanation of man's proclivity for religious persecution. Under the rubric "Barbaries Chrétiennes," Voltaire totaled up a minimum of 9,468,800 persons killed by Christian zealots, a cliometric exercise that listed the religious massacres century by century.[4] When the psychologists' domino theory was credited, then fear brought psychic suffering to the religious adept, the suffering brought on an inner rage, and the rage vented itself in ruthless persecution of heretics and unbelievers. Instead of religion being viewed as the solace of mankind, this sacred disease was identified as the source of the greatest miseries. Again, it was Diderot, in his novel *La Religieuse,* who illustrated the sexual perversities and cruelties generated in the unnatural atmosphere of a convent, where women in the name of religious devotion denied themselves the fulfillment of elementary passions. The fear of God drove men to the extremes of absurdity and madness: They lacerated their own flesh in exercises that bewildered most of the *philosophes* and to which their subtlest reasoning could offer no clue. Trenchard in his natural history of superstition had showed an awareness that some kind of religious self-punishment—specifically monks' "scarifying their backsides"—might in fact produce sexual pleasure. But such allusions to flagellation as a means of sexual gratification were rare. In general, self-inflicted tortures as part of religious observance were considered inexplicable lunacy and dismissed as such.

That asceticism was unnatural and ascetic practices brought about consequences opposite to those intended had frequently been remarked upon by doctors of the Renaissance, and no less a man than Isaac Newton condemned the mortifications of anchorites, who in their futile attempts to banish lewd and lascivious images from their minds were only driven to dwell on them the more. One of his manuscripts dissected their predicament with insight: "[D]esire was inflamed by prohibition of lawful marriage, and . . . the profession of chastity and daily fasting on that account put them perpetually in mind of what they strove against. . . . By immoderate fasting the body is also put out of its due temper and for want of sleep the fansy is invigorated about what ever it sets it self upon and by degrees inclines towards a delirium in so much that those Monks who fasted most arrived to a state of see- ing apparitions of women and other shapes and of hearing their voices . . . in such a lively manner as made them often think the visions true apparitions of the Devil tempting them to lust."[5] Similar psychological diagnoses of the chimeras consequent upon what we would today call sensory deprivation can be found among many of the *philosophes*. That an overscrupulous punitive censor provokes a rebellious reaction in a man's breast, a commonplace among present-day clinicians, was a widespread perception of the *philosophes*' literary psychology, though they never quite reified the unconscious.

II

One of the presuppositions of the eighteenth-century distinction between true philosophical religion and popular religion was a dogmatic opinion about the nature of perception among primi- tives. Many of the missionaries to the heathen, both Catholic and Protestant, in trying to explain away their lack of success in mak- ing converts resorted to the excuse that primitive peoples had no capacity for abstract ideas, a notion that had wide currency in seventeenth- and eighteenth-century anthropology and that lived on well into the twentieth century, until it was discredited by Claude Lévi-Strauss. This attempt of the international mission- aries propagating religion among savages to justify to the home office their own incompetence was in line with the judgment of the *philosophes* that ordinary people, Christian or heathen, were psychically unable to reach the exalted level of members of the Academy either in religion or philosophy because they were de- ficient in an aptitude for abstraction.

In his early reflections on religion, John Locke had explained idol- and saint-worship as a result of the almost ineradicable ten- dency of common people to concretize. Savages knew the names of objects, not of abstract qualities, and for ordinary people God had to be portrayed in a manner comprehensible to the senses. In Locke's wake, David Hume saw that most men could not maintain themselves on the abstract level of monotheism, but had to fall back like the tides into polytheistic doctrines in which each god had a particular control over a specific natural element that was associated with him. Catholic saints and their worship played the same role—they were tailored to fit the perceptual capacities and understanding of ordinary humans. Calvinist fire and brimstone sermons had to picture graphically the torments of hell in order to be effective. Popular religion in all times and places, pagan or Christian, was likely to be cursed with the same concreteness. The people were incapable of moving back in their reasoning, through a long linkage of causes and effects, to a primary cause, but had to make up some immediate tangible cause, a saint's image or a relic, and impute to it powers it did not possess. The generalization that *philosophes* had made about gradations in the fear syndrome was repeated with respect to concreteness of perception: The more ignorant a person was, a child, for example, the less his capacity for abstraction. What applied to the individual had occurred in the history of the race: Benighted savages concretized; higher stages of civilization acquired a capacity for the abstract. Women were likely to have no propensity for abstraction and to be more addicted to superstitious religions, an idea that has become taboo in our lifetime, but was an eighteenth-century self-evident truth.

Even Hume's philosopher had only partially outgrown a deficiency in the capacity for abstraction. When he donned his philosophical robes and thought rigorously and scientifically he might for a time be emancipated from the concreteness syndrome. But in ordinary, everyday life he too was subject to making concrete analogies and failed to display the abstract attitude necessary for a philosophical religion. Some of the Deists had a rather crude physiological conception of why men did not hold firm to the idea of God. Primitives seemed to have soft brains, and erroneous impressions could readily write themselves on this substance and distort their natural, pure reason, making them a prey to imaginary monsters. False religion was thus a natural offshoot of the physiopsychology of error.

In the latter part of the eighteenth century theories on the ori-

gins of religion assumed a more sophisticated shape. Charles Dupuis's *Origine de tous les cultes* (1795), in a revival of ancient Stoic
doctrines and seventeenth-century ideas, saw practical religion, including Christianity, as a degenerate form of scientific knowledge
about the universe. The masses, because they could not remain on
the requisite high level of true theory about the nature of things,
corrupted the findings of ancient philosophers and, like the Egyptians, fell to worshiping animals and other low things whose symbolic meaning they could no longer read. The idea of religion as
primitive science opened the possibility of a new true religion of
science, a conception with a long future history.

Another idea that flourished in a later epoch was the sexual interpretation of religion. After the introduction of epics from
India, along with erotic Indian sculpture, there was a minor attempt to discover the genesis of religion in a symbolic rendering
of human sexual activity. (There had been ancient doctrines to
this effect.) But while this inspired some pornographic interest in
collecting certain types of Greek and Roman coins, it was not a
widely diffused psychological scheme of interpretation.

III

One school of eighteenth-century thinkers, while committed to the
prevalent idea that popular religion had its origins in fear, held
that this was necessary for the maintenance of the state and civil
society. In a variation of the ancient Critias doctrine, they contended that fear of the gods prevented men from committing secret
crimes and thus served the interests of the state by helping to maintain order. Voltaire's "footman's religion" was tinctured with this
psychology—though the forthright atheist Holbach shocked his
contemporaries with the assertion that it was the state's gallows
and not the gods that deterred men from crime. In *Dieu et les
hommes* Voltaire asked rhetorically: "What restraint, after all,
could be imposed on covetousness, on the secret transgressions
committed with impunity, other than the idea of an eternal master
whose eye is upon us and who will judge even our most private
thoughts?"[6]

In its most militant form, anticlerical analysis of religion, while it subscribed to the fear theory and the idea of the ordinary man's incapacity for abstract thought, tended to concentrate on the lust for power as the most compelling drive behind the propagation and maintenance of institutional religions. The power-lust could be imputed either to kings or cliques of priests, who conspired to impose deceptions and false beliefs on the mass of the people. Not all individuals were equally wily and power-hungry. Most of the guileless merely did as they were told by the more astute, who acted out of self-interest, that eighteenth-century theoretical catch-all. There were mastery and riches and pleasure to be gained by those who directed the religious plot and enforced a monopoly of knowledge for themselves while they kept the people in darkness. This plot theory of the origins and sustenance of religion was shared by Voltaire and Holbach and received its final form in Condorcet's *Esquisse* on the progressions of the human mind. Ordinary people acted out of habit. Once their ancestors had been instructed by priests about the commandments of the gods, they were transmitted from generation to generation and remained unaltered, except when a few extraordinary persons broke through the shell of custom and made an attempt to perceive relationships freshly. It was then that priests in alliance with tyrants moved to destroy the heretics who had brought new perceptions into the world, and the mass of the people, terrified of suffering a similar fate, continued their religious performances like docile sheep.

Through their monopoly of knowledge, the priests not only amassed wealth and power, but while preaching ascetic behavior to the people, they could themselves enjoy all manner of sexual gratifications. Seventeenth- and eighteenth-century stories that repeated classical themes—Denis Vairasse's *History of the Sevarambians,* for example—featured wicked priests who forced innocent virgins into sexual relations by making them believe they were having converse with a god. The sexual advantages gained by priests through knowledge imparted in the confessional became a stereotype of the anticlerical crusade. Ordinary human stupidity, played upon by the craftiness of a few tyrants and their priestly cohorts, offered a complete explanation of most religious behavior. "In a word," Holbach pontificated in *La Contagion sacrée,* "[sovereigns] had to rule by prejudice backed up by force. Caprice was their only law, a power without limits the object of all their desires. And having become the cruelest enemies of their peoples they had to look for supernatural means to hold them in subjection, to divide them, to prevent them from resisting the evil they had to endure. . . . Only religion could perform these miracles."[7]

IV

Most of the theories of the psychology of religion were advanced by the enemies of revelation, who converted doctrines formulated to isolate true religion from fanatical enthusiasm into battering rams against the whole orthodox religious structure of society. In the second half of the century, however, a new view of religion sprang up among a number of seminal writers that was, so to speak, a negation of the eighteenth-century negation. Rousseau, Hamann, and Herder, and even orthodox Catholic apologists in France, began to view religious performances in a new, positive light, and to bolster this changed attitude toward popular and institutional religion a new psychology of religion was evolved.

The meaning of Rousseau's religion is open to a wide variety of interpretations; but in one of its aspects it introduced great novelty. For Rousseau, religion in its very essence was not to be understood as a social utility, the core of Montesquieu's apology; nor was it a historical phenomenon that at best had served to mollify the cruelty of barbarian invaders, as Gibbon at one point contended; nor was it merely a necessary bridle or restraint on the wild concupiscence and inherent evil nature of man, as the orthodox apologists of all religions believed. Religion was an expansive effusion of the emotions of love and benevolence that represented the best and the noblest in man's nature. Rousseau's Vicar of Savoy saw religion as the mainspring of virtuous feeling and action. Religion was a vital part of the education of man because it brought to the fore his naturally benign sentiments. It was a positive drive, a *ressort,* not a mere *frein,* or checkrein. This religion of the heart needed no elaborate institutional forms; it could be inspired in man by the beauties of nature, and, far from being the special province of the learned and the scientific, had its great-est chances of development in the natural feelings of untutored peasants. The Vicar exhorted Emile: "Behold the spectacle of na-ture; listen to the inner voice. Has not God spoken it all to our eyes, to our conscience . . . ?"[8] The whole Rousseauistic concep-tion of human nature fostered this simple religious belief. Only aristocrats and corrupted savants were atheists. The religion of the people was natural and spontaneous—at least before it was spoiled by arts and sciences.

On the eve of the Revolution, the Rousseauistic religion, strangely enough, penetrated the works of official popular Catholic apologists, and ceremonials were devised that harmonized with this conception of religious belief as a natural stimulus to virtue. The spreading cult of the rose-wreath, in which villagers, by gen-eral consent, awarded a prize of virtue to a local virgin—a cere-mony attended by the lord, the clergy, and royal officials—was a manifestation of the new view that among the peasantry of France true religious feeling was still alive, whatever might be happening in the salons. "I feel within me the love of the good and I give my-self up to it," preached the Abbé Bourlet de Vauxcelles, a court-cleric sent up to Normandy to participate in a rose-wreath fete. The very titles of popular works of apologetics gave evidence that a new psychology of religion was in the making. The Abbé Adrien Lamourette—the later initiator of a kissing game during one tense revolutionary assembly—had published in 1788 Les Délices de la religion.

Catholic apologetics, as if in answer to the arguments of those psychologists who saw religion as born of fear, or religion as a con-sequence of power-lust, or religion as an attribute of brutish igno-rance, were propagating a new romantic view—religion as the natural spontaneous gift of all good and feeling people. This may have been a last-ditch attempt of the compromised church of the Cardinal de Rohan to save itself; but it turned out to be a prefigu-ration of a whole new psychological interpretation of religious behavior that was to flourish in the nineteenth century and is far from dead today. Whether this facile sentimentalized religion bears any but the most tenuous relationship to the scriptural and historical religions of Judaism and Christianity is, as my master Hume would say, "exposed to some more difficulty."

Related to Rousseauism, the interpretation of religion that was being prepared on the other side of the Rhine by one of the fathers of German Romanticism, Johann Gottfried Herder, opened an entirely new mode for understanding the genesis and worth of religion in civilization. Instead of being an evil growth it again became the heart of culture. As part of his philosophico-historical outline of the history of the *Volk*, Herder saw the birth of the religion of a people as its most spontaneous creative moment. Responding to the inspiration of the physical environment in which it was created, religion was the primal molder of a national soul, the wellspring of its whole history. To be sure, Montesquieu had conceived of religion as a vital element in fashioning the spirit of a nation, but in his rationalist frame religious creativity was not endowed with anything like the driving force that Herder granted it. The new view of religion that was nourished in the Germanic world was a vigorous denial of the accumulated theories that English philosophers and French *philosophes* had developed in the course of the eighteenth century. When Hume's *Natural History of Religion* was translated into German, Herder quickly picked it up and focused not on its anticlerical implications but on the skeptical philosopher's admission that religious emotion was spontaneous. Hume had marked it a secondary emotion derived from fear; Herder rejected the fear theory and stressed the sentiment itself. He stood on their heads all the psychological perceptions of the *philosophes;* and religion, instead of being denounced as the major source of human depredations and cruelties, was suddenly turned into the font of all creativity in art and literature. By the end of the century, in a counter-Enlightenment movement from the Germanic world, the psychology of ordinary religion was transformed from an offensive weapon against established religion in the hands of the *philosophes* to a defense and a bulwark of Christianity.

Thus the period of the Enlightenment left behind two very

different psychologies of everyday religion, depending upon whether their underlying model of man was a terror-stricken savage or a loving creature full of gratitude for the bounties of nature. Both theories have enjoyed a long history in Western society. What they had in common was their rendering of divine revelation and the God of commandments as either supererogatory or cruel.

4 A GODLESS HISTORY

WRITING his autobiography at the height of his eminence, Edward Gibbon could look down patronizingly, yet fondly, on the fledgling author of the *Essai sur l'étude de la littérature*, a French piece published by a young Englishman in 1761: "The obscurity of many passages is often affected . . . the desire of expressing, perhaps a common idea, with sententious and oracular brevity—alas, how fatal has been the imitation of Montesquieu! But this obscurity sometimes proceeds from a mixture of light and darkness in the author's mind; from a partial ray which strikes upon an angle, instead of spreading itself over the surface of an object. After this fair confession, I shall presume to say that the *Essay* does credit to a young writer of two and twenty years of age, who had read with taste, who thinks with freedom, and who writes in a foreign language with spirit and elegance."[1] Much of the *Essai* had been completed in 1759, before his Anglican father allowed him to return from his exile in Lausanne, where he was recuperating from a scandalous conversion to Catholicism. This mixed bag of reflections on the worth and uses of the study of ancient literature contained more penetrating revelations about his image of himself as a man with the vocation of a historian than he later recognized. Doubtless the mature Gibbon would have retracted some of the grandiloquent generalities and surrounded others with cautions, but his practice as a historian never departed far from the model of the perfect *historien-philosophe*—the term is Gibbon's—delineated in this youthful exercise. He had the good fortune to fulfill an early ideal in a great work, realizing in the course of his own life the generous hopes he had once expressed for a scholar whom he expected to become the English Muratori: "a man of genius at once eloquent and philosophic who should accomplish in the maturity of age, the immortal work which he had conceived in the ardor of youth."[2]

I

The term *philosoph-historicus* is an old one going back to Jean Bodin, though it is doubtful whether Gibbon had read the *Methodus, ad facilem historiarum cognitionem* (1566) at this point in his career and it appears in none of the catalogues of his libraries. Voltaire had not yet made popular the phrase *philosophie de l'histoire,* which he first adopted as the title of a pseudonymous work in 1765, and to my knowledge Gibbon at no time employed it. When in the *Essai* he set forth the considerations that should govern the philosophical historian (a word combination reasonably current by then), he was acting independently, as though oblivious of predecessors, with the confidence of a bold young innovator breaking new ground in the conceptualization of secular history writing without providential guidance.

Gibbon made a vital distinction between the creative genius in a field of human endeavor and the plodder: The former was always a philosopher. Granted that the purpose of any historian was to collect facts and deal with causes and effects, the truly philosophical historian had to be endowed with a unique capacity: to single out those facts that dominated a whole system of interrelationships. He used the word "system" loosely to connote a nexus of relations within a spatiotemporal perimeter, not a rigid philosophical theory. Gibbon had imbibed the prejudice of the age against the *esprit de système,* and while he would write history *en philosophe,* he was no builder of philosophical structures. Certain critical facts, few in number, were the main springs of action (*ressorts*) that put everything in the system into motion. Genius philosophical historians who were "capable of distinguishing these types of fact in the vast chaos of events and drawing them forth pure and unalloyed" were rare creatures. The facts they focused upon were not necessarily the sonorous formal pronouncements of historical figures or the most dramatic events of history. On the contrary, *petits traits* (minor characteristics) and apparently insignificant customs and manners might hold within them the great secrets that propelled nations and ages into movement. In the *History of the Decline and Fall of the Roman Empire* Gibbon was to demonstrate that as much could be learned about the Romans from their behavior in circuses as from their orations in the forum. Bossuet's Christian God manifesting His will through the magnificent acts of grand historical agents was nowhere visible.

From the outset Gibbon conceived of the historian as a man charged with unveiling, with probing the innermost recesses of past societies. This sense of mission might be related psychologically to a longing for primal knowledge and a metaphysical anguish about where he came from, to fantasies about his ancestry, to boyhood images of an *Ile de la félicité,* and to the womblike libraries in which he enclosed himself in London and Lausanne— but the attempt would lead into strange byways. Gibbon himself preferred facts not deliberately reported by the actors as more likely to convey essential information than public decisions of historical protagonists. It would be grossly anachronistic to say that he had a theory of unconscious acts, but he was creeping up on the idea. "There is no façade in the performance of trivial actions. One undresses when one expects not to be seen. But the curious inquirer tries to penetrate the most secret hiding-places."[3] Clinicians have found that voyeurism and the fear of being seen, passions not uncommon among some of our greatest historians and archaeologists, are often combined in the same person. Tacitus, Gibbon's ideal philosophical historian, was doubtless the model for his search into the arcanum of the Roman Empire, but such a probing may also have had deeper roots.

While Gibbon pleaded for the importance of small details, he categorically rejected the Pascalian Cleopatra's nose thesis; there were no great effects from minor causes. Details, however, far from being devoid of significance, were crucial to the philosophical historian who could interpret them as revelatory of the profound springs of a nation's action. Young Gibbon dared to challenge the great d'Alembert, who in one of his essays had casually proposed a radical way of dealing with the fast-growing accumulation of un-assimilated data in all branches of science that threatened to en-gulf society: At the end of each century, d'Alembert counseled, mankind should select those that added to positive knowledge and throw the rest away. On the contrary, Gibbon argued with youth-ful vigor, no fact however trivial should be destroyed because one could not know what a Montesquieu would make of it. Montes-quieu had discovered the spirit of the laws, not in the declama-tions of popes and kings, but in the multiple minor characteristics of nations. This esteem for a full knowledge of all things in the past, without discrimination, which went along with a vindication of erudition, had a limited number of enthusiastic proponents in the eighteenth century, Vico among them; but their voices were feebler than the dogmatic Cartesian condemnation of history as an obfuscatory burden on the mind in its search for truth.

There is no evidence that Gibbon knew Vico's work at this period of his life, though later he may have gotten a whiff of his ideas through Muratori, the Italian historian whose achievement he greatly admired; still, there are a number of provocative paral-lels between the views of the greatest eighteenth-century theorist of history and the greatest historian of the age. For Vico, societies spoke in their gestures, their banners, their poetry, their customs—these were the materials of the New Science. Gibbon did not trans-form the detail into a symbol, but for him, too, no fact was ever without import—its meaning needed only to be fathomed.

Gibbon's ideal philosophical historian had attributes that were later associated with the Romantics. He had to be capable of pene-trating the mentality of every nation and people, even of following an Iroquois's mode of reasoning. Gibbon may not have had a Vichian conception of the *mente* of successive ages as embodying different modes of perception and he never hypostatized *tre spezie di nature*. Whatever distinctions he recognized among different ages and nations, there was only one human nature, modifiable under varying conditions. But the idea that a historian, by enter-ing into an alien mentality that reasoned falsely, could neverthe-

less discover a signal truth about human nature was already prominent in the *Essai* and underlay Gibbon's later attempt to grapple
with the theological disputations of the early Church. A theologian's mind was as penetrable as an Iroquois's.

By negation, Gibbon made apparent his own views on the potency of both systematic rational purposiveness and caprice in human behavior. While other historians had portrayed men as either
trop systématiques or *trop capricieux*,[4] he saw them as an amalgam
of reason and caprice. Demonstrating the rational purposiveness
of great personages, perhaps the major historiographical preoccupation of the time, was not his exclusive concern, because he had
observed that expressed intent usually concealed men's real passions and penchants. People were driven to vicious conduct by
passion and they then justified their actions by subtle rational-
izing. The dominant forces in history were emotive, not reasonable. In an even more striking passage (unconnected with his
description of the philosophical historian), Gibbon naughtily con-
fessed: "I like to see the judgments of men take on color from their
prejudices, to cast my eye on those who do not dare to draw, from
principles they recognize as just, conclusions that they know to
be correct. I like to take by surprise those who abhor in the barbarian what they admire in the Greek, and who call the same story
impious in a pagan and holy in a Jew."[5] Reviewing the parade of
emperors and churchmen in the six volumes of the *History*, he
rarely missed an opportunity to savor his malice by showing up
the hypocrites who covered their baser desires with legal or theological mouthings. But he played holier-than-thou only in extreme
cases. For the most part, he recognized the fickle superficiality of
his own reasonings in the face of desire. On one occasion he flip-
pantly wrote his friend Holroyd (later Lord Sheffield): "As I used
to reason against riding, so I can now argue for it; and indeed the
principal use, I know in human reason is, when called upon, to
furnish arguments for what we have an inclination to do."[6]

While history was the science of cause and effect, it was the part
of the philosophical historian to look for general and determinate,
not particular, causes. Gibbon excluded the providential as a pri-

mary cause beyond his ken and, at least in later utterances, the presumed absolute laws of history or universal historical systems, the most common of which was still the worn-out formula of the four monarchies derived from the Book of Daniel. The Bossuet whose writings had been instrumental in Gibbon's brief conversion to Catholicism had lost his sway over the apostate. With youthful abandon Gibbon proposed a "philosophical history of man" that would yield a knowledge of general, though finite, causes. He called for a new Montesquieu to carry out this project; and who was this Montesquieu but Gibbon himself? "He would reveal for us [these general causes] controlling the rise and fall of empires; successively assuming the features of fortune, prudence, courage, weakness, acting without the concurrence of particular causes, and sometimes even triumphing over them."[7] This paragon among philosophical historians would follow the operation of profound causes in long-term trends, whose slow but certain influence changed imperceptibly the face of the earth. The idea that events happen insensibly, a notion which became a tic in the later volumes of the *History,* had made its appearance in the phrase *sans qu'on puisse s'appercevoir.*[8] Manners, religion, and whatever depended on opinion were the primary fields in which these secret causes left their mark, without anyone's being consciously aware of the fundamental changes society was experiencing.

The key word in Gibbon's philosophico-historical reflections in the *Essai* is *ressort,* one of the widely current, baffling terms of eighteenth-century Anglo-French thought that are so difficult to understand precisely. It has obviously mechanistic overtones, but it was commonly applied to individual and social action by writers who by no means subscribed to the conception of an *homme-machine. Ressort,* by analogy to a clock or an automaton, since Montaigne had come to mean a moving cause, an energizing force, generally hidden, that created movement.[9] In the mid-eighteenth century, medical terminology was beginning to mingle vitalistic with mechanical ideas in explaining the life-giving force in animal bodies, and such notions were adapted to the study of history and society. Gibbon's "spring" is eclectic and fuses mechanistic and

vitalistic connotations without his having had much contact with
contemporary medical controversies.

Gibbon's remarks about *ressorts* in the *Essai* can be illustrated
from the *History,* though he did not repeat the sweeping theoretical imperatives of the earlier work. His magnificent choice of 1,300
years of the history of the physical entity that was the Roman Empire was at once extensive and finite, a universe of discourse that
allowed him to avoid both the teleology of the theologian's universal history and the amorphousness of contemporary academic
scholarship with its disparate minutiae. Within this world of the
Roman Empire, we can now discern in the *History* three subordinate and relatively autonomous systems of relationships—to resur-
rect the terminology of the *Essai*—that have definable inner
springs of action: the Roman, the Christian, and the barbarian.
And we can watch Gibbon shift his spotlight from one system to
another with consummate skill, as he unfolds the drama of Rome's
decline—the theatrical analogy is eminently appropriate for this
inveterate playgoer.

Gibbon was specific about the pervasive forces that drove each
of these determinate systems. The Roman ruling passions—their
"springs"—were military glory and civic virtue, which impelled
them to extend the Empire to the uttermost frontiers of barbarism,
a stock eighteenth-century explanation of Roman hegemony. The
exercise of military prowess was in the end a major element in the
breakdown of the Roman system. Gibbon is the grand historian of
the working-out of the ultimate consequences of these *ressorts* in
the physical and moral realms: Imperial overextension led to the
loss of a sense of liberty among nations in the Roman world, the
breakdown of administration civil and military, and the corruption of morals. The springs of the Christian system were of a different character. Zeal and fanaticism—ugly things—in the propagation of faith, passions derived from the Jews, and a promise of
life after death brought about Christianity's spiritual triumph
throughout the Roman Empire and at the same time undermined
the civic virtue of the Romans. Religious disputation and persecution that further weakened the cohesion of the body politic were

inherent in the fanatical nature of Christianity itself, so different from the tolerant spirit of Roman paganism. And finally there was the system of the barbarians, whose *ressorts* were the most elementary and primitive. They were driven by fear of starvation, their natural cruelty, and an innate need to wander. The interplay of the three systems, reified as if they were dramatis personae in a tragedy, presented the "greatest, perhaps, and most awful scene, in the history of mankind."[10]

I doubt whether Gibbon sat down and deliberately sketched any such total pattern in advance—we know that the *History* grew like Topsy and that the three stages in the publication of the six volumes, 1776, 1781, and 1788, marked disjunctures in his thinking—but the achievement of this type of configuration involving the discovery of a few concealed springs and an exposition in detail of how they persistently operated over a long period of time was already the goal of the young historian-in-the-making back in 1761.

Gibbon described other overlapping or derivative systems of relationships, the separate universe of the thousand-year history of Byzantium, for example. Here a system was formed that had no original motive drive of its own. Its lifeless hands held on to a portion of the territories of the Romans and its voice parroted the ideas of the Greeks. It was dominated by no other passion than the mere maintenance and preservation of its inheritance. This was a closed system in a state of stagnation, without *ressorts*.

But what were the origins of the particular "springs" themselves in any system of relationships? Except for a few remarks about geography, Gibbon was not very enlightening on this score: Remote and primary causes, reminiscent of providential history, were not his field of investigation. Sometimes the springs of action appear to resemble innate components of national character; at other times they seem to be extensions onto the body politic of the prevalent psychology of the ruling passion in individuals.

Gibbon was familiar with the long catalogue of forces and active agents that in Montesquieu's theory fashioned the *esprit* of a nation, an idea not alien to his own concept of *ressort*. For the neophyte in search of a historical model, the narrative had to demonstrate the interpenetration of these elements and their mutual reinforcement, creating a unity. In entries of his journal in the sixties, he explicitly rejected the work plan of the French historiographer-royal, Voltaire, exemplified in *The Age of Louis XIV*, where each type of human activity had been isolated and compartmentalized in a separate chapter under a heading. To write history *en philosophe* would mean establishing interconnections and tracing their operation through time. Montesquieu's structuralist tendencies, which our own contemporaries appreciate, were flaws in Gibbon's eyes, and he violated chronological order only in the last books of the *History*, where the barbarians become the major protagonists, for aesthetic and literary reasons.

A philosophico-historical problem that preoccupied Gibbon in the *History* is only touched upon in the *Essai*, the phenomenon of progression and decline in the arts and sciences and in the dominion of empires. Gibbon did not entertain the abstraction of the idea of progress or perfectibility, but he dwelt upon one aspect of the concept, as he tried to define his position in the literary quarrel of the ancients and the moderns, a hangover from the seventeenth-century disputation. Wrestling with the preferences in 1761, he came out nowhere in particular. While modern Europeans might surpass the ancients in the politics of domestic tranquillity, the present peaceful situation of society was not favorable to the genius of poetry, in which the ancients excelled. Rousseau's thesis of the Second Discourse (without being specified) was feebly denied: "The sciences they say are born of luxury; an enlightened people will always be corrupt. I do not believe it."[11] There is a dilution of Rousseau's pessimism in Gibbon's confidence that sciences will make manners more gentle and act as a countervailing force to the tendency of luxury to make men languid. The analogy he drew from the *Iliad*, however, hardly turns him into a progressionist: The sciences (and he means knowledge, not merely the physical sciences) are likened to prayers that fly over the earth in the wake of injustice to mollify the fury of this cruel divinity. Gibbon did not yet accept anything remotely resembling the proposition of Turgot's *Sorboniques* of 1750—the inevitable continuation of progression somewhere on the globe despite local setbacks. Most of the latter part of the *Essai,* in which the "origins of pagan religion" are discussed, is so thoroughly immersed in the language and conceptions of David Hume's *Natural History of Religion,* published in 1757 (again, the text is not named), that one detects some agreement with the Humean alternativity doctrine of "flux and reflux" in human belief. Gibbon's analysis was often painfully shallow, as he attributed the flourishing or decay of one or another art or branch of knowledge to a mere change of fashion.

The *Encyclopédie* had underplayed historical and literary subjects in favor of mechanics and positive science, and in adopting the Baconian schema had depressed history to the low estate of the art of memory. At this period of his life, when he was trying mightily to justify the study of ancient literature and combat the denigration of history among many of the reigning Encyclopedists, Gibbon refused to be impressed by the much-vaunted triumphs of physical science. There is an undercurrent of hostility on the part of this defender of literary culture against the physical scientists with their pretensions to extending over all forms of human knowledge the spirit of geometry, "that imperious queen who, not content with ruling, proscribes her sister sciences, and declares all reasoning hardly worthy of the name that is not concerned with lines and numbers."[12] Young Gibbon went so far as to contest the idea that the scientific improvements of the moderns necessarily represented an advance over the ancients, and his vindication of the study of ancient literature was intended to preserve it by proving that its utility was at least as great as that of the new physical sciences. Only rather late in life did Gibbon take to auditing lectures on astronomy and chemistry, and whenever there was occasion for mentioning mathematics he promptly shied away from it. His appreciation of technology probably grew with time, as we shall see; but a certain ambivalence about it persisted. Young Gibbon was a man of one culture and his concept of civilization did not necessarily require scientific and technological triumphs. When he wrote of civilization he surely implied a widespread use of the mechanical arts and the observance of legal norms and civility in social intercourse among members of his class; but high civilization still meant, first and foremost, literary-philosophical culture. Only three of the one hundred and thirty-nine pages in the 1785 subject catalogue of his Lausanne library are devoted to physical sciences.[13]

II

Though the mature Gibbon was in touch with the major currents of thought on both sides of the Channel—his Anglo-French education was comprehensive in most branches of history, literature, theology, and philosophy—two writers, one French and one English, who viewed history philosophically played the principal roles in his intellectual life and help to locate him in the spectrum of prevailing ideas, Montesquieu and Hume. Adam Ferguson, with whom he was acquainted personally, is less of a direct influence than an interesting parallel, though Gibbon reviewed the *Essay on Civil Society,* and the *History* echoes some of Ferguson's apprehensions about the loss of virtue among overpolished peoples. Voltaire, who had received Gibbon without being particularly impressed by the young Englishman, left his imprint on the style and wit with which the theological controversies of the early Church were treated. Both of course had drunk deeply of the patristic sources and reveled in turning their pious traditions upside down. Gibbon's Chapter 15, "On the Progress of the Christian Religion," which aroused the orthodox, bears more than passing resemblance to Voltaire's *Dieu et les hommes* (1769), with its chapter headings on "Des causes des progrès du christianisme" and "De la fin du monde et de la résurrection annoncée de son temps," as well as its statistical digressions on *barbaries chrétiennes.*

Montesquieu's *Considérations sur les causes de la grandeur des Romains et de leur décadence* and the *Esprit des lois* were major legacies from the previous generation. When Gibbon was writing the *Essai,* Montesquieu had been dead four years, but his fame was still growing in both the French and English worlds. In the *Essai,* Montesquieu was the modern constantly cited with favor. Gibbon even applied to himself the closing phrase of the preface to the *Esprit des lois,* "And I too am a painter," for which Montesquieu acknowledged a debt to Correggio. Such reservations about Montesquieu's thesis as Gibbon entertained arose from his own commitment to the chronological method of exposition and from occasional misgivings about Montesquieu's promulgation of historical generalities as if they were laws of nature rather than "determinate" generalities limited in time and space[14]—though it would not require too diligent a research to compile from the *History* observations on human conduct and the motivations of men that appear to be universal, after the manner of Montesquieu. Contemporary critics were quick to recognize that some of the underlying conceptions in the *History*, the explanations for the decline, were not very different from Montesquieu's two causes for the decadence of the Romans. Montesquieu, however, had concentrated primarily on the evil consequences of extension, whereas Gibbon introduced Christianity as a principal, an open affront to religion that Montesquieu would have been reluctant to risk. While there are obvious similarities between Montesquieu's theory of the different ruling passions of nations and Gibbon's idea of the profound, deep-rooted causes that were the springs of action in a society, the scale of Gibbon's six volumes was of an entirely different order from Montesquieu's elegant little treatise. And if Gibbon adopted a number of Montesquieu's generalities, they were almost commonplace by the latter part of the century. The *Encyclopédie* had summarized them in an article on the Roman Empire, and the basic formula—"it sank under the weight of its own greatness and power"—would re-echo in Gibbon's text.

It was Hume's influence that was the more pervasive in the formation of the philosophical historian. Hume too was of the older generation, but he did not die until after the publication of the first volume of Gibbon's *History* and the bestowal of his accolade upon the new literary knight. Gibbon treasured praise from the dying Hume above all other appreciations, and he kept quoting the words of approval to all his correspondents. Though there is no evidence that the tightly reasoned *Treatise on Human Nature* meant much to him, we know from his journal that he read the *History of the Stuarts* in the early sixties, and arguments from *The*

Natural History of Religion and other essays were cited a number
of times in the footnotes of the first volume of the *History*. But it
was no single work of Hume's alone that dominated Gibbon; it
was the man and his writings in their totality that were congenial
to him and set Hume above all other contemporary philosophical
writers. We know of the personal acquaintance of the two men, of
Hume's securing a clerk's job in the government for Gibbon's life-
long friend Georges Deyverdun, of Hume's brief contribution to
the abortive venture of Gibbon and Deyverdun into literary journalism, the *Mémoires littéraires de la Grande Bretagne,* which ran
for two issues, of Gibbon's combing Hume's essays for information
as well as spiritual guidance. But beyond all this, close affinities
can be found in what these two corpulent bachelors considered
to be moral and civilized. Moreover, neither Hume nor Gibbon
had any doubt that it was the responsibility of the historian to act
as a moral judge. Hume wrote an inquiry into the principles of
morals and Gibbon, less formally philosophical, though he never
spelled out the principles or criteria of his judgment, also had a
reasonably well-defined schedule of the virtues and vices of men.
The ideal values in Hume's *Enquiry Concerning the Principles
of Morals,* the combination of the *utile* and the *dulce,* were also
Gibbon's. There is not a virtue Hume extolled that Gibbon would
have failed to embrace. If one ransacked the writings of Hume and
Gibbon and drew up a list of positive and pejorative characteristics cited by each, one record would mirror the other. Gibbon
constantly measured historical personages by these standards and
then established history as the world court of judgment. "Whatever subject he has chosen," Gibbon wrote of the important office
of the historian, "whatever person he introduces, he owes to himself, to the present age, and to posterity, a just and perfect delineation of all that may be praised, of all that may be excused, and of
all that must be censured."[15] One of his more pompous utterances.

To win Gibbon's plaudits, men of the past had to exhibit the
same kind of civilized behavior as contemporary gentlemen. They
could not be addicted to anything—women, the hunt, wine, honors, godliness. They had to favor a policy of peace and recon-

ciliation. They were obliged not to act dishonorably, break their word, deceive, be hypocrites, delude themselves. His heroes were men who promulgated codes of law, established order, fostered the arts and sciences, extended mercy to the vanquished. In the end, his estimates of private individuals and his descriptions of historical persons became interchangeable counters. He was always playing with chiaroscuro effects. He juxtaposed virtues and vices to present a credible human being. But to meet with the approval of the philosophical historian sitting as the Great Judge the balance of a man had to be weighted in the direction of the eighteenth-century virtues Hume had identified in the *Enquiry*. On the death of a Lausanne acquaintance, Saloman Charrière de Sévery, Gibbon wrote: "Sévery was indeed a very valuable man: without any shining qualifications, he was endowed in a high degree with good sense, honour, and benevolence, and few men have filled with more propriety their circle in private life."[16] This sort of man represented for Gibbon the epitome of civilization. And it did not matter much that he was "a little *ennuyeux*."

The civilized way as Gibbon recognized it had been embodied in two societies, the Roman (with side glances at the Greek) and his own British (with side glances at the pre-1789 French). For both Hume and Gibbon, civilization was a fragile thing. It was forever being assailed by the forces of darkness—religious fanaticism and mass barbarism. Gibbon had no more admiration than Hume for the pretensions of the religious to a sublime experience or for the grandeur of the heroic virtues. Both were content to rest with what Hume, with a touch of self-mockery, called the aldermanic virtues. This does not mean that Gibbon never approached the fire—occasional passions flicker briefly and two friendships lasting for decades bordered on love; but once he was free from his father, his overt equilibrium was only rarely upset by onslaughts of emotion. Deep anxieties existed, but his biographers have thus far failed to probe beneath the mask of complacency.

Like his master David Hume, Gibbon stood for civilization defined in terms of the class and culture in which he was born and bred. Though he was the grandson of a director of the South Sea

Company, he identified himself with the style of the aristocracy of Britain and France and the "bourgeoisie" who were the nobility of the Swiss republics. If the report is true that Gibbon and Deyverdun were Freemasons walking in the footsteps of the Huguenot aristocrat who was Deyverdun's uncle, a known Freemason, the values of aristocratic Freemasonry that had abandoned the sword for the virtues of benevolence and peace were those of Gibbon.[17] (There was a list of regular lodges of Freemasons in his library.)[18] He could be accused of inconstancy in love, in religion, and in political party allegiance—and he was sensitive to the charges of being a turncoat in all three areas—but he would have been profoundly dismayed if he had been found wanting in the virtues that both he and Hume associated with civility. If civility is set at the heart of his intellectual and emotional existence, his work and his life show a remarkable degree of harmony, despite the "contradictions" in the man Gibbon, of which he was conscious and which he sometimes flaunted.

Gibbon's commitment to civility is evident throughout his philosophical history of the Roman Empire. It opens with that grandiose description of the geographic and political landscape of the Age of the Antonines. Here is civilization triumphant—liberty and law prevailed, and there was an adequate policy for their preservation. Though the picture has been labeled a Tory utopia, Gibbon was keenly aware of its dark side as well as its light. But under the Antonines a greater number of men enjoyed the benefits of peace and tranquillity, freedom from hunger and arbitrary rule, than ever had before. Life in eighteenth-century Britain was in a similarly optimal condition. Gibbon felt that he himself lived under a regime that was a counterpart to the Age of the Antonines. What he wrote about Rome before the decline could be applied to Britain without straining: "The temperate struggles of the patricians and plebeians had finally established the firm and equal balance of the constitution; which united the freedom of popular assemblies, with the authority and wisdom of a senate, and the executive powers of a regal magistrate."[19] Roman civilization had been destroyed by forces inimical to the "middling way" of Hume and Gibbon, by Christianity and barbarism.

Internally, the strength of Rome had been sapped by the fanatical religion of those ecclesiastical disputants who invaded the balanced culture of the Romans, epitomized in Cicero and Horace. Gibbon avoided discussing Christ and the Apostles themselves; he was writing a secular, not a sacred history. But without casting doubt upon the truth of the Gospel, he described the Christians of the proselytizing and theological ages as betrayers of the values of civilization. They lied and fabricated documents, ceased to be tolerant, persecuted one another over matters of no consequence. Utility and comfort were abandoned for self-torture and frenetic devotions; monkish virtues were exalted to the highest degree; and the ways of civilization were lost. Amid the Christian zealots only the Roman consul kept his poise. On the face of the record, the barbarians were the immediate instrumentality of the destruction of Rome; but they were not the primary force. The spiritual subversion of the Roman world had come first, and was accelerated after the union of Roman power with Christianity. The barbarians were almost unconscious agents obeying mere instinct, and in a way they were no more blameworthy than brute beasts. Tacitly refuting Saint Augustine, who had exonerated the Christians from responsibility for the fall of Rome, Gibbon charged the self-righteous fanatics of the City of God with demolishing the civil society of the City of Man.

Turgot, Gibbon's contemporary and Hume's friend, in his unpublished writings had seen the Church as the great spiritual institution that ultimately tamed the barbarians, and thus he could turn the succinct world history presented in the *Sorboniques* into a theodicy. Gibbon's brief apology for Christianity at the end of Volume 3 is unconvincing: "The pure and genuine influence of Christianity may be traced in its beneficial, though imperfect, effects on the barbarian proselytes of the North. If the decline of the Roman Empire was hastened by the conversion of Constantine, his victorious religion broke the violence of the fall, and mollified the ferocious temper of the conquerors." These sentences seem hardly more than a sop to those who had attacked him for irreligion. (Edward Gibbon was not above encouraging a prospective French translator, the litterateur J. B. Suard, to tone down the language of the notorious Chapters 15 and 16 of Volume 1.[20] He gave similar advice to his actual translator, Leclerc de Sept-chênes, who was secrétaire du cabinet du Roi—which led to the tale that King Louis XVI himself had had a hand in the work.)

The destruction of Roman culture on the part of the Christian ecclesiastics could not be forgiven. Compared to the religious fanatics, the barbarians had virtues or at least the seeds of virtue, especially a love of liberty, which when tamed by the revived law of the Romans again restored civility. Mankind had paid dearly for the hegemony of churchmen, and never again should it countenance their rule over society: That was one of the morals of the story. Gibbon was not the implacable enemy of religion; he would merely keep it in its place, the civil place it had occupied in the Roman world before the advent of Jewish and Christian zealots. After his conversion back to the Church of England, Gibbon would defend the institution as necessary to civilized existence—a utilitarian argument, already present in Montesquieu, that was in consonance with Gibbon's reputed Freemasonic affiliation. Hume's chronicle of the evil contagion of enthusiasm in his history of the Stuarts had a profound influence on Gibbon's world-historical view. The seventeenth-century "enthusiasts" had made an assault on the recovered civilization of antiquity, and it was fortunate for mankind that they had been worsted so that eighteenth-century Britain might exist.

III

Though Gibbon still considered himself an *historien-philosophe,* in 1776, on the eve of a century that witnessed the appearance of the major European systematic philosophies of history (old style), he was untouched by this kind of theorizing. He was a grand periodizer, and, in accordance with the inescapable formula of European thought, in the preface to the first volume of the *History* he divided the account of the collapse into three segments; but he evinced no interest in stadial theories. Vico's *Scienza Nuova,* whose last version appeared seven years after Gibbon's birth, was no more within his sphere than within that of the overwhelming number of European intellectuals. The German thinkers Herder and Kant and the Swiss Isaak Iselin, who published philosophies of history during Gibbon's lifetime, did not come to his notice (he knew no German and at most was acquainted with German thought through his friend Deyverdun, who had translated *Werther*). Suzanne Curchod's daughter, the redoubtable Madame de Staël, had not yet invaded Germany, returning with her Teutonic trophies. The currents of intellectual influence generally moved from West to East in the eighteenth century, rarely the other way. Gibbon did know of the efforts of Englishmen and Frenchmen who speculated on the origins and growth of civilization, such as Goguet, Court de Gébelin, Boulanger, Monboddo, but the closest Gibbon seriously approached to the early history of mankind was a flirtation with Isaac Newton's new system of world chronology. Gibbon's seal was adorned with Plato's head, but like many literary gentlemen of the age he did not appreciate metaphysics ancient or modern, neither Plato nor Leibniz, whose philosophy he at one point summarized in vulgar clichés. Sometimes I doubt whether he really followed the labyrinthine arguments of the great theological controversies he ridiculed so brilliantly.

When he came to maturity, Gibbon at first turned his back on the grand design he had outlined for himself in his youth. It was as if he took fright and swung in the opposite direction, in his first projects seeking refuge in such little worlds as a life of Sir Walter Raleigh, or the history of the liberty of the Swiss, or the history of the republic of Florence under the Medici. His final settling on a daring subject, the decline of the Roman Empire, represents at least a partial return to philosophical history. As he struggled through the maze, he tried to recapture the general goals he had outlined in his youth. The conclusion of the first volume (he then thought he had come to the end of his project), which raised in a forthright manner the problem of the causes of the decline, harked back to his early quest for general and determinate causes. His

presentation was probably spiked with a desire to shock his readers, much as he would entrance the ladies in a salon with his
wicked *boutades.*

By 1781, fortune having smiled upon him, Gibbon became more
adventuresome, and at the end of Volume 3 he again picked up
philosophico-historical questions that were preoccupying European intellectuals, above all the decline and fall of civilization in
general. It would have been difficult to avoid the issue. Many of
the illustrious *philosophes* in the later 1770s had begun to feel that
their society was on the brink of a decline; it was not only Diderot's advancing age that led him to identify himself with Seneca,
though the plain fact that the *philosophes* were getting old and
beginning to die off was certainly an element in the formation of
this sentiment. In his last years Diderot often expressed the idea
that the renascence of the arts and sciences, that flowering of civilization which had reached its zenith with the Encyclopedists, had
run its course. The internal difficulties of the French monarchy
were patent, and the corruption of morals was widely portrayed in
France, often in a new type of literature. Gibbon read the novels
of Restif de la Bretonne, the "Rousseau des ruisseaux"—Restif is
even mentioned in the autobiography[21]—and Laclos's *Liaisons
dangereuses,* along with his normal diet of works of erudition.
(The de Sade whose work Gibbon knew was the author of a life of
Petrarch and paternal uncle of the "divine Marquis.") The chron-
icler of the moral decadence of the Romans was not impervious to
the new emotional tonalities that were being sounded in France.
Those chaste and playful relationships of the Lausanne girls and
boys in their literary societies that were the delight of his youth
and the proper fetes at Voltaire's Ferney, in which Gibbon had
participated, were no longer à la mode.

The insurgency of the American colonists created political anxieties in Britain which, though different from those inspired by
French "decadence," affected Gibbon more immediately. The Gibbon who had come to live his *History* far more profoundly than
the gentleman of fashion was prone to admit could not escape the
analogy between Rome and Britain. Sitting in Parliament, he

fancied himself a Roman senator; and he was conscious of his partiality toward the old paganism. He had accepted his historical calling with a measure of reluctance, or at least ambivalence—the gentleman at first did not want to be marked as a professional writer—but once the die was cast he was possessed by his subject. It became an intensely personal history. The distance he achieved artistically from the events and characters he portrayed was often a self-consciously Horatian pose.

Even before Gibbon had chosen his subject, he was struck by parallels to Rome's fate, and once he became immersed in the *History*, associations thrust themselves upon him wherever he turned: in the exclusiveness of the Berne "bourgeoisie," adamantly refusing to extend the franchise despite the threat of civil strife, even as the old Romans had; in the British Empire during the War of American Independence; in the France of 1793 confronted by the "new Barbarians"—his phrase; and in the persons of great men—Leibniz failing despite his genius because, like Rome, he had overextended himself. Sardonically Gibbon made comparisons between the gradual decline of excruciating pain during one of his periodic seizures of gout and the demise of Rome. Perhaps he saw a type of Roman decline in his own family's waning fortunes, from the grandfather who was a director of the South Sea Company, through his profligate father who had wasted his inheritance.

The daily events of the War of American Independence, 1775–1783, during the very period when Gibbon was writing a major part of the *History*, were constantly raising in his mind a history of the decline of the British Empire. Parallel lives and parallel histories were part of the literary canon. The Abbé Mably, Gibbon's competitor in historiography, had composed a parallel history of the Romans and the French (though he later repudiated the grossness of the analogy).[22] Gibbon never actually wrote a parallel history of the British and the Romans, but the comparison was in the background of his thought. No nineteenth-century positivist, he was untroubled by the reality that when one depicts past ages one draws them, "sans s'en appercevoir," after models

that are before one's eyes.[23] His letters during this decade are full
of the resemblances between Britain and Rome. Often they were
a subject of wit. "As for the man of letters and the statesman," he
wrote to Georges Deyverdun, "rest content with the knowledge
that the declines of the Two Empires, the Roman and the British,
are advancing at an equal pace. I have, to be sure, contributed
more effectively to the former. In the 'Senate' I am still just as you
left me, *mutus pecus*." [24] But there was genuine concern beneath
the jesting.

Gibbon was not in favor of the war against the American colonies because the vision of a society wasting itself in foreign military adventures called up the Roman analogy. "What will be the
resolutions of our Governors I know not, but I shall scarcely give
my consent to exhaust still farther the finest country in the World
in the prosecution of a War, from whence no reasonable man en-
tertains any hopes of success. It is better to be humbled than
ruined," he wrote to his stepmother.[25] In fact, of course, he did
nothing except vote with the government like a placeman and
write a hack's memorandum against French intervention. When
the victory of the colonists occurred, Deyverdun's view of British
prospects darkened, while Gibbon assumed a guardedly ambiguous tone, as he had in Volume 3 of the *History*, published in 1781
when British defeat was already taken for granted. Reporting his
most intimate thoughts to Deyverdun on May 20, 1783, after a long
interval, Gibbon recalled that his friend had little liking for great
power, either England's or Rome's. In any account of modern
history there would have to be talk of the decline of empires, and
Gibbon believed his friend would find him in general agreement
with him once he left Parliament and again became an "homme
philosophe et historien." All the same, he thought the British fall
had been gentler than that of the Romans. After failure in war
and an inglorious peace, Britain still had emerged with its civilization intact and the wherewithal to live in contentment and happiness.[26] Following Deyverdun's death, Gibbon was alone in the
paradise of Lausanne and he realistically foresaw the inconve-
nience of old age; but for society he could hardly conceive a more

favorable balance of social forces than existed in his day in Britain or Switzerland. The question provoked by the similitude of Britain and Rome, however, was not wholly laid to rest.

IV

The apprehensions of many eighteenth-century *philosophes* over the internal decay of their society were reinforced by the haunting fear of another barbarian irruption from the heart of darkness that would overwhelm Western civilization in a repetition of the awful spectacle of the fall of the Roman Empire. Tartary was usually assigned as the point of departure for the invasion, though sometimes it was intentionally left vague or declared to be unknowable. The *Avertissement* to the eighth volume of the *Encyclopédie* is perhaps the *locus classicus* for the expression of this anxiety. "It is possible that a revolution [from the context it is clear that Diderot meant a massive outburst destructive of civilization] whose seed may even now be burgeoning in some remote region of the world or secretly incubating at the very center of civilized countries should break out with time, overthrow cities, again disperse peoples, and bring back ignorance and darkness." After the publication of the *History*, Condorcet, last of the *philosophes*, continuing to grapple with possible negations of *progrès indéfini*, in his prognostication of the future progressions of the human mind reflected that "only one *combinaison*, a new invasion of the Tartars from Asia, might impede this revolution."[27] (Here the fluid word refers to the diffusion of Enlightenment throughout the globe.)

In the *Encyclopédie*, Diderot's response to his own fear of a recrudescence of barbarism either from within or from without was a magnificent boast uttered in a moment of triumph when his task was nearing completion: "All will not be lost, if a single copy of this work survives." Condorcet's manuscripts are dotted with practical projects for encapsulating all knowledge into an encyclopedia written in a universal, hieroglyphlike language and burying it in a fireproof repository, protection in case of geological cataclysms as well as political upheavals; and in the *Esquisse* (1795) he argues at length the proposition that the eventuality of a barbarian invasion is henceforth impossible. Gibbon prefigured much of Condorcet's reasoning, though he avoided dogmatic terms such as "impossible" and customarily modified bold assertions with adverbs of doubt: "perhaps," "probably," "possibly," "essentially."

At the end of Chapter 38 of the *History,* in a section entitled "General Observations on the Fall of the Roman Empire in the West," Gibbon tried to dispel the gloom of Britain's fading prospects by dismissing the question of her decline in favor of the broader problem of the chances of survival of European civilization as a whole. And here, putting aside the discomfiture of the patriot, Gibbon offered his fellow men the consolations of a philosophical historian—though he provided himself amply with loopholes and escape clauses, lest he be one day judged a false prophet. These "Observations" are not an integral part—they are surely not a summary—of the three volumes he had completed by 1781, and his remarks might be viewed as an independent response to the contemporary world. Gibbon thought his task was finished in 1781, and he was making reflections *en philosophe.*

The query of an absent adversary was simple: If Rome succumbed, what was there so extraordinary about modern European civilization that it might escape a similar destiny? In making reference to Scipio's confession to Polybius that as he watched Carthage burning he recalled the vicissitudes of human affairs and wept as he envisaged the future calamities that would befall Rome, Gibbon bore witness to the weight of the ancient Greek historian's contention that all states and empires were subject to decay. In the face of the overwhelming experience of the nations, the burden of proof that modern Europe was in some way an exception to the common rule was on the philosophical historian. The arguments are Gibbon at his most Gibbonian.

He advanced three "probable" reasons why Europe should now feel secure, in contrast with the tragic inevitability of the fall of Rome, a structure crumbling under its own weight.

The first reason was based upon a consideration of human geography. Under the Roman Empire, the territories beyond the Rhine and the Danube had been sparsely populated and occupied by roaming tribesmen; once the impetus of a Chinese attack against the Huns set everything into motion, one tribe of barbarians pushed another through the great vacant spaces—a sort of eighteenth-century version of our domino theory—until the tribesmen overflowed onto the territories of Rome. In Gibbon's day, fortunately, the whole of the northeastern part of the Continent was occupied by the civilized Russian Empire of Catherine II, darling of the *philosophes*—remnants of Kalmucks and Uzbeks were no longer to be feared—and this extensive settled territory served as a buffer for the republic of Europe. But Gibbon had no sooner made the argument than he withdrew a few paces. "[T]his apparent security should not tempt us to forget, that new enemies, and unknown dangers, may *possibly* [italics his] arise from some obscure people, scarcely visible in the map of the world."[28] There was, after all, the precedent of the Arab conquests. And in a footnote Gibbon indicates that barbarian movement in the other direction was not excluded: "Nor will I venture to ensure the safety of the Chinese empire."

The second reason was related to the contrast between the imperial constitution of the Roman Empire, which had crushed the freedom and spirit of individual client nations and thereby made them more vulnerable, and the numerous independent kingdoms and republics that constituted modern Europe, where there were restraints on the abuses of tyranny and even the most defective governments had some sense of honor and justice. The Europeans, though an agglomeration of polished nations, had not been allowed to fall into somnolence because of the constant emulation among themselves in the acquisition of knowledge and in the practice of industry. Should barbarians once again invade, Gibbon raised the prospect—in some respects absurd—of a united, energetic Europe, comprised of the most varied elements, joined to repulse them. "If a savage conqueror should issue from the deserts of Tartary, he must repeatedly vanquish the robust peasants of Russia, the numerous armies of Germany, the gallant nobles of France, and the intrepid freemen of Britain. . . ." Having made this oratorically optimistic point, he again became circumspect—

"who, *perhaps* [italics mine], might confederate for their common defence."[29] But then he bounded back: In case of danger there was always America to which the survivors could flee in "ten thousand vessels"; the Atlantic Ocean would serve as an ultimate bulwark of European-civilization-in-America against barbarian aggressors. Though writing when the political separation of the colonies from Britain seemed, at least to Gibbon, a foregone conclusion, he soothed his countrymen with the expectation that the manners of Europe would be preserved and the English language diffused over an immense continent.

The third comfort derived from revolutionary transformations in the military art that had resulted from the invention of gunpowder. To this technological superiority—a mainstay of the debate between the ancients and the moderns at least since Bacon—Gibbon added a few new considerations. He had frequently observed in the *History* that despite Roman excellence in devising new instruments of war, the valor of the soldiers fell off with the progressive decline of laws and manners. But modern science and technology had effected changes in the defensive capacities of Europe of a qualitatively different order: Industry could now make European cities impervious to barbarian conquest even if the military virtue of the polished Europeans should be found wanting. Once again Gibbon receded from this blanket assurance, but this time by taking refuge in a paradoxical turn of thought. The barbarian invaders might conceivably be victorious over the fortified European cities, but in order to achieve this triumph they would have to become so skilled in the use of sophisticated European techniques of warfare that in the process they would cease to be barbarians, and so civilization would win after all. Though succumbing to conquest might be its fate, European civilization would not be annihilated. He cited the example of Russia: Advances in the science of war had there been accompanied by improvements in civil policy under Catherine II. This form of reasoning, which saw civilizing processes deriving dialectically from the war-lust of power-hungry despots, was running through Europe and was even adopted by Kant in distant Königsberg, in his famous essay of 1786 on universal history, to strengthen his confidence in the moral improvement of mankind.

But what if all these speculations on the immediately favorable situation of Europe should somehow prove to be vain? To allay his own uncertainties, Gibbon raised his sights and took an anthropological view of the development of mankind. His broad-gauged analysis of the "improvements of society" appeared to break the bounds of the historical in support of the presumption that total collapse was no longer possible. Dimensions were enlarged even beyond the European continent, as he examined the progressions from the condition of the human savage over four thousand years earlier to man's present state of civility. The process had had slow beginnings and then redoubled velocity, a changing tempo that Turgot had remarked upon. It was not rectilinear and had experienced moments of rapid downfall. Though Gibbon inherited the Renaissance belief in the vicissitudes and he was reluctant to prognosticate the height to which the human species might aspire in its advance toward perfection, nevertheless— and this is as far as he would go at this point in the direction of the Turgot-Condorcet convictions—"it may safely be presumed, that no people, unless the face of nature is changed, will relapse into their original barbarism." Even the Romans had not fallen so far as to renew the "human feasts of the Laestrygons on the coast of Campania." To promise his fellow men freedom from anthropophagy was no resounding affirmation of the certain progress of civilization, but it was further than many thinkers of the older generation of Anglo-French culture were prepared to venture.

Much of the detailed reasoning about the "improvements of society" recalls Turgot's ideas, still in manuscript when Gibbon wrote, and what Condorcet would publish a few years after Gibbon's death. (The only work by Condorcet in Gibbon's library was a hostile consideration of Pascal, *Eloge et pensées de Pascal*, 1778, though some far-out progressionist prophecies were available in Mercier's *An 2440*, also in his library.)[30] Direct evidence of "influence" from these French *philosophes* is lacking, but the resemblances are plentiful. Most striking is Gibbon's division of the improvements of society into three different types, along with an estimate of the diverse fortune each was likely to experience in the course of the ages. Turgot had made a similar diagnosis of the varying fortunes of the progressions, intellectual-scientific, artistic, mechanical, and moral. Gibbon lumped together poetic and scientific genius and made both the product of mere chance and spontaneity. Turgot, though he would have agreed as to the rarity and inexplicable character of genius, had a well-nourished theory about the relations of the state of society and the capacity of a genius to fulfill himself that was not approached by Gibbon, who on the whole seemed to feel that nothing much could be done about the marvelous, unaccountable appearances of genius—its incidence was not affected by historical forces. (Yet in the *History* itself he had sometimes maintained a contrary position.) But industrial accomplishments, the cultivation of the arts and sciences, which were common experiences of mankind, and the laws were less independent phenomena and as a consequence were subject to the complex machinery of the social order. They could be destroyed by violence or allowed to fall into gradual decay. Achievements in these realms did not always endure, and Gibbon was silent on the subject of their necessary accumulation. The only improvements of society about which he expressed confidence were the mechanical arts, whose preservation was dependent neither upon genius nor upon the whole fabric of society. Elementary techniques learned in families and villages in the course of time were the most durable acquisitions. Turgot made a similar appraisal of the continuity of mechanical progression even in the darkest ages of mankind, though his emphasis was somewhat different from that of Gibbon, who was concerned primarily with survival. "Private genius and public industry may be extirpated," Gibbon wrote, casting a last dubious look on the great achievements of European civilization, but the "hardy plants"—he was referring to the mechanical arts—"survive the tempest. . . ."[31] Turgot had written on the usefulness of war in spreading the arts; Gibbon held a similar view. "Since the first discovery of the arts [I believe that in this context he referred chiefly to the useful or mechanical arts], war, commerce, and religious zeal have diffused, among the savages of the Old and New World, these inestimable gifts: they have been successively propagated; they can never be lost," he wrote in one of his rare, unqualified affirmations.

I cannot demonstrate that Gibbon was acquainted with Turgot's ideas on progress, though the two men met in Paris. Memoirs on Turgot's life and thought were published by Dupont de Nemours in 1772 and by Condorcet in 1786, but the actual texts of the *Sorboniques* and the *Recherches sur les causes des progrès et de la décadence des sciences et des arts, ou réflexions sur l'histoire des progrès de l'esprit humain,* the *Tableau philosophique des progrès successifs de l'esprit humain* (1750), and many reflections on philosophical history remained mere "projects" and did not appear during Gibbon's lifetime. Though David Hume was well aware of his friend Turgot's conceptions, which he rejected in their correspondence, Gibbon's personal ties to Hume were not close enough to suggest oral transmission. Turgot's ideas remain parallels, not documented influences, though often the similarities are arresting. Gibbon's Chapter 53 on the stultification of Greek culture during the thousand-year reign of the Christian Byzantines is a good illustration of Turgot's thesis that the archenemy of progress, a sickly tendency toward repetition and sameness, was responsible for sinking whole societies into a rut. "It is not error that is opposed to the progress of truth, not wars and revolutions that retard the progress of governments, but softness, stubbornness, routine, and everything that leads to inaction," Turgot had written in *Recherches sur les causes des progrès et de la décadence des sciences et des arts.*[32] His favorite example of intellectual stagnation resulting from a closed monopoly was the mandarin class in China, though he extended his censure to all sects, philosophical and religious, in Egypt, Greece, and Babylon, and he was suspicious of the clique spirit among the authors of the *Encyclopédie,* to which he had contributed. Gibbon placed the blame for the stagnation of Byzantium on its isolation and the absence of competition both within the empire and with other societies. "In all the pursuits of active and speculative life, the emulation of states and individuals is the most powerful spring of the efforts and improvements of mankind."[33] As a consequence of Byzantium's addiction to the mere repetition of what had been received from the ancients, Gibbon issued his famous verdict: "In the revolution of ten centuries, not a single discovery was made to exalt the dignity or promote the happiness of mankind. Not a single idea has been added to the speculative systems of antiquity, and a succession of patient disciples became in their turn the dogmatic teachers of the next servile generation."[34]

Before propositions demonstrating the inevitability of progress were set forth in Turgot's *Sorboniques* and Condorcet's *Life of Turgot,* it is hard to find members of the Anglo-French philosophical school who staunchly maintained an absolute position. A pre-Revolutionary thinker such as the Abbé Raynal might be quite radical in his reformist zeal, believe that the mission of the age was to wipe away the debris of the old order, and yet conclude, as he did in the *Histoire philosophique* (which Gibbon knew well), that the changes effected would not be enduring. Raynal likened the rise and fall of nations to turns of the weather vane; to Leibniz the movement resembled the ebb and flow of the tides; and both Voltaire and Diderot, in their casual, unsystematic way, saw the dominion of nations increasing and diminishing without rhyme or reason. The Abbé Galiani perceived the rise and fall of civilization as phases of the moon, a recurrent natural phenomenon from which there was no escape. Such analogies are far less intricate than some of the Renaissance doctrines of the vicissitudes, but they appear to have satisfied the philosophico-historical needs of major thinkers in the early and middle periods of the Enlightenment. When Turgot and Condorcet offered proofs of the inevitability of progression in the scientific and the moral realms, not merely an alternativity of progress and decline, they were opening up a very different prospect.

Gibbon resists being compressed into either a progressionist or a cyclical mold, and he surely was not a regressionist—which exhausts the three fundamental possibilities Kant later outlined in his *Disputation of the Faculties*. Gibbon accepts the proposition that the relative balance of power and intellectual supremacy among the European nations will continually shift. Only when he views European civilization as a whole does he begin to approach the Condorcet prophecy. After all his tergiversation one is prepared to receive Gibbon into the fold of the partial lapsarians, to describe his stance as a middling, normative, *philosophe* position, when the concluding sentence of Chapter 38 makes a giant leap into the realm of limitless, unbounded progress. "We may therefore acquiesce in the pleasing conclusion, that every age of the world has increased, and still increases, the real wealth, the happiness, and perhaps the virtue, of the human race." The attentive reader, hardly prepared for any such enthusiastic adherence to the idea of progress in its full-blown Turgot-Condorcet version, is left bewildered. He can only be grateful for the introduction of the saving "perhaps" before Gibbon, carried away by his own rhetoric, binds every age of the world to progress in "virtue."

In France and England it was the dominant philosophical opinion, whether Montesquieu's or Rousseau's, Diderot's or Hume's, that all states and empires had to endure periods of decline and regression. Though Gibbon went along with the negative argument of Turgot and Condorcet that declension was not inevitable, to my knowledge he never forthrightly subscribed to the positive one, except in that lone sentence concluding Volume 3 of the *History*, which seems almost like the attempt of the salon conversationalist to end on an amiable and pleasing note.

v

A year after the appearance of the last volume of the *History*, there was an eruption of "new barbarians" in France, and along with some English fellow fanatics they were menacing the whole of Europe, including the British Empire. For once Gibbon's Olympian serenity abandoned him, and he exhorted all good Englishmen to resist the French contagion. During this period there is no text of his marked by the simple conviction that the British imperial defenders of civilization would be more successful in the long run than their ancient counterparts. After 1789, when Gibbon thought about the future it was with misgivings; there were innovators in the Swiss republics and mobs in Bristol.[35] When Gibbon reported Necker's exaltation of Britain as the first and perhaps last asylum of liberty, the historian of the decline and fall of the Roman Empire was standing at Burke's side against the fanatics of the French Revolution. He announced himself a Burkean in everything; he even forgave Burke for his superstitions. Gibbon was ready to resort to any act of policy that would strengthen the moral fiber of his countrymen, even to the point of helping draft and signing a solemn petition of loyalty that would join men of all parties in support of the British constitution. Before he was shaken by the events of the French Revolution, the *historien-philosophe* who had incisively diagnosed the gradual, insensible forces that brought about the decline and fall of Rome over the centuries would not have given great weight to such verbal prophylaxis.

By the 1790s Gibbon was beginning to fear the destruction of France and with it a danger to all of European civilization. He viewed the affairs of France with a crescendo of alarm. On September 25, 1789, he had written to Lord Sheffield: "That country is now in a state of *dissolution*."[36] On December 15, 1789, "the honestest of the Assembly" were characterized as "a set of wild Visionaries (like our Dr. Price) who gravely debate and dream about the establishment of a pure and perfect democracy of five and twenty millions, the virtues of the golden age and the primitive rights and equality of mankind which would lead in fair reasoning to an equal partition of lands and money. How many years must elapse before France can recover any vigour, or resume her station among the powers of Europe? As yet, there is no symptom of a great man a Richelieu or a Cromwell arising either to restore the Monarchy, or to lead the Commonwealth."[37] By February 23, 1793, he wrote to Lord Loughborough of the threat to the whole of Europe: "[A]s a friend to government in general I most sincerely rejoice that you are now armed in the common cause against the most dangerous fanatics that have ever invaded the peace of Europe—against the new Barbarians who labour to confound the order and happiness of society, and who, in the opinion of thinking men, are not less the enemies of subjects than of kings." [38] Gibbon in Lausanne was ready to go into mourning over the execution of Louis XVI, but he was "afraid of being singular." [39] When two requirements of appropriate civilized behavior clashed, Gibbon's more enthusiastic resolves always crumbled. The *historien-philosophe* maintained his outward social equipoise to the end.

Gibbon's descriptions of the dangers of extension, the destructive effects of highly centralized limitless power on the internal spirit of the body politic, the loss of civic virtue that accompanies the complex machinery of a far-flung military establishment, the hazards of luxurious excess, the constant drives of fear and hunger among the "barbarians," are reasonably faithful mirrors of our own condition and his evocations have a macabre fascination for us. The Gibbonian Atlanticists among us, still suffering from his Europocentric illusions, cannot read without a *frisson* one of his many final summations, "the reflection of a philosophic mind": "[T]he decline of Rome was the natural and inevitable effect of immoderate greatness. Prosperity ripened the principle of decay; the causes of destruction multiplied with the extent of conquest, and as soon as time or accident had removed the artificial supports, the stupendous fabric yielded to the pressure of its own weight. The story of its ruin is simple and obvious; and instead of enquiring *why* the Roman empire was destroyed, we should rather be surprised that it had subsisted so long." [40]

We are tempted to ask again Gibbon's awesome question in the famous Chapter 38—and to respond with his characteristic ambiguousness: If the Roman world collapsed, what is to keep European civilization from decline and fall? There are times when few of Gibbon's consolations seem pertinent and some of his reassurances sound hollow. The acquisition of sophisticated weaponry by new centers of civilization or by peoples recently fashioned from tribes Gibbon in his parochialism would have considered savage or barbarian does not appear to have exerted any immediate civilizing influence upon them—that is, if we join him in his narrow, eighteenth-century, English upper-class definition of civilization.

But perhaps in the long run these weapons may indeed turn out to be the only civilizing force, a prospect that is a rather corrosive ointment for the self-inflicted wounds of the older civilizations. There are, alas, no great buffer states to contain the barbarians, unless the middle one of the three great powers that encircle the earth be regarded as a buffer between the other two at any given time. The new Christians among us—whoever they may be—can be identified by their fanatical zeal, not by the mollifying influence of their faith. Emulation among the civilized nations in the acquisition of knowledge continues at an accelerated pace, though there seem to be new dangers associated with its procedures that Gibbon never dreamed of. The sciences, which in his earliest work he saw as mitigating the fury of injustice, now have unloosed powers capable of good and evil that join the furies as often as they quiet them. Should war among the great nations erupt, there is even grave doubt about Gibbon's ultimate solace to his civilized contemporaries—that men would not return to the state of anthropophagy.

5 ISRAEL IN THE CHRISTIAN ENLIGHTENMENT

THIS meditation on Israel in the Enlightenment passes over the mass of eighteenth-century Christian believers who dutifully performed their prescribed religious ceremonies, while in secret practicing pagan and primtive rites. It is engaged, rather, in converse with priests and bishops, doctors of divinity, professors of theology and ancient languages, and writers in various conditions of independence—literary men who lived on their estates or survived by their wits, *philosophes* who published journals and were occupied in remolding what Thomas Jefferson called the opinion of mankind. To this heterogeneous group a simple question was posed: What did they make of the ancient God of the Jews who lived among them, sometimes legally as in Holland, more often under murky arrangements as in France, but always on the margin of society? During the period of the Enlightenment there was a growing curiosity about the Jews and their God, as He and His chosen people were becoming more visible.

The responses constitute a reappraisal of ancient Judaism by Christians, many of whom were in the course of divesting themselves of the complex theological and dogmatic raiment of their own ancestors. The nature of Judaism—not only the physical existence of the Jews—has always been a prickly subject for Christianity. In the age of the Enlightenment, new ways of ending the ambiguous position of Judaism in the bosom of Christendom were proposed. An attempt among certain literate elements of European society to cut the umbilical cord that had bound Christianity to Judaism from the moment of its origin was the most conspicuous break with tradition. More radical thinkers, reaffirming the historical tie with great fanfare, deliberately painted Judaism in gruesome colors in order to undermine the foundation of their own Christian religion. Others conceived of a new relationship between Judaism and Christianity that allowed for their coexistence through a redefinition of the nature of religion itself.

I

The revolutionary character of the re-examination of Judaism may be communicated more fully if set against the background of Christian views of ancient Judaism that still prevailed on the eve of the Enlightenment.

In seventeenth-century Christian universal history, the binding of Jewish and Christian experience was taken for granted. The survival of the Jews was conceived as an eternal punishment for the sin of deicide or as an everlasting witness of the Crucifixion. In the eyes of Catholic theologians, Jews had been burned by the secular arm after an inquisition not because they were Jews but because they were relapsed Christians or demons luring Christians to apostasy. The major state religions of Western Europe—Catholic, Lutheran, Anglican, and Calvinist—taught that, although the Jews in their stubborn blindness had balked at accepting Jesus as the Messiah, there was one continuous sacred history from Adam through the present; with the insertion of pseudepigrapha like the books of the Maccabees and the inclusion of the histories of Josephus, it was possible to join the Old and the New Testaments in an unbroken narrative.

The universal history composed by Bossuet, the official churchman of Louis XIV, was really a history of Judaic experience joined to the history of Christianity, with the Roman Empire subordinate to the future needs of the Church, and the Chinese or other pagan histories ignored as having no intrinsic worth. This drove Voltaire in his passion to overturn Bossuet's universe and spitefully to start his world history with the Chinese. Anglican divines of all species—and there were many—adhered to a Bossuet-like central narrative. Humphrey Prideaux in his *Old and New Testament Connected* revealed the coherence of the divine plan in its totality.[1] Isaac Newton, who devoted thousands of manuscript pages to the subject, many of them now in Jerusalem, fortified the structure with a new method of astronomical dating based upon the precession of the equinoxes and with proofs that in the great civilizing enterprises of mankind—architecture, the laws, the belief in the true God, writing—the Hebrews had preceded all other nations chronologically. Homer had derived his wisdom from Moses, as Clement of Alexandria had affirmed. In the seventeenth century there were many idealized portrayals of ancient Israel as the progenitor of Christianity. The Abbé Fleury's *Les Moeurs des Israélites* (1681) made of it a pastoral utopia that was a pendant to Fénelon's *Aventures de Télémaque*. Moses was the great legislator of antiquity, far superior to the *nomothetai* of the Greeks.

In the political debates of the sixteenth and seventeenth centuries in northern Europe, it was common to draw upon Old Testament biblical texts to find sanction for either monarchy, democracy, or aristocracy in a Christian polity; James Harrington in his *Oceana* even discovered a mixed establishment of the three in Moses' structuring of the Hebrew republic.[2] In the lively, often scratchy, political pamphleteering of the English Civil War, there was a complete identification of the Commonwealth saints with Israel, and men busied themselves drafting law codes that would incorporate the rules of Deuteronomy down to the last tittle, or almost. The theocracy of Massachusetts was meant to be a literal implementation of the Mosaic code, with a few exceptions. The glorification of the Sabbath as the only day of the Lord and the rejection of Christmas as the residue of a pagan festival were symbolic of the Puritans' self-image as Israelites.

The hope of effecting the conversion of the Jews and moving on to the millennium was a common Protestant expectation that lasted well into the eighteenth century. Judah Monis, a rather enigmatic wandering Jew who came from someplace in the Mediterranean, ended up at Harvard, was given a degree in 1722, and was appointed an instructor in Hebrew after being duly baptized.

His formal sermon celebrating that event dealt with the interpretation of the proof texts in the Old Testament on the coming of
Christ, supported by rather obscure rabbinic citations.[3] Increase
Mather, as President of Harvard College, had often lectured on the
mystery of the survival of the Jews. Among Calvinists it was only
the failure of the Jews to accept Christ that stood in the way of a
total approval of Jewish experience. Lutheran tradition was more
tightly bound to the Judeophobia of its founder.

Christian preoccupation with Judaism became more intense in
the Protestant world as the Old Testament, translated into the
vernacular, was widely diffused. It was discovered to be veritably
bursting with figures and types of the New Testament. Few verses
could not be adapted to demonstrate a prefiguration of sacred
Christian history that was later fulfilled. Catholic theologians had
been engaged in such practices since the time of the Church
Fathers; and if the texts illustrating concordances between the
Old and New Testaments, such as those of Joachim of Fiore, are
no longer commonly read, the idea of their linkage may be quickly
grasped through visual examples. A medieval tapestry in the
Metropolitan Museum in New York depicts on the lower level
scenes representing the seven sacraments, while on the upper level
are parallel Old Testament events: The anointment of David is a
type for the sacrament of extreme unction.

Cotton Mather in his *Magnalia Christi Americana* of 1702 still
saw a virtuous contemporary divine in New England as a Bos-
tonian incarnation of an Old Testament figure. It was no burden
on a young member of the Massachusetts Bay colony to go about
with a weighty name such as Shearjashub. In the wilderness of
New England the colonists were reliving the sufferings of the
Israelites. And a bit of rabbinic *gematria*—the translation of words
into numerical equivalents—applied to prophecies in Daniel and
Revelation, which conformed to each other, sustained the dating
of the Second Coming.

The weaving together of pre-Christian Judaism and Christianity was constant in the centuries before the Enlightenment. It was
perhaps most complete in the Swiss, Dutch, and English (including

the American) scholarly worlds of the seventeenth century. And if hard-working believers could not themselves research the rabbinic commentaries for types, foretellings, and prefigurations, their pastors—usually chosen for their learning as well as their eloquence—poured something of this knowledge, garnered from the works of Christian Hebraists, into the willing and unwilling ears of their auditors, who were subjected to a continuous round of sermons on the Holy Sabbath, on special fast days, and on days of thanksgiving.

II

Christian Hebraism of the seventeenth century occupies a corner in the cemetery of baroque learning, that magnificent age of scholarship when the production of a hundred volumes in a lifetime was considered a feat, but not an unsurpassable one. The grand folios of the Christian Hebraists were produced by the presses of Amsterdam, London, Venice, Leyden, Rome, and Frankfort, and are now preserved in university treasure rooms, rarely disturbed by intruders. Modern scavengers have hardly bothered to pick the bones of these worthies or plagiarize them, let alone savor the content of their works. An occasional essay on them has appeared, but few have ventured to encompass the writings of John Selden, John Lightfoot, John Spencer, and Edward Pocock in England, Johann Buxtorf, father and son, in Basel, the Dutchmen Jan van den Driesche, Adriaan Reeland, Antonius Van Dale, Pieter van der Cun, Wilhelm Surrenhuis, Philipp van Limborch, the heterodox Père Richard Simon in France, or the scholar who published in Leyden and bore the sonorous name Constantin L'Empereur van Oppick. The bibliographical zenith of this outpouring of Christian Hebraism was reached in the Catholic world with the publication of Giulio Bartolocci's four-volume *Bibliotheca Magna Rabbinica de scriptoribus, & scriptis hebraicis* (1675–1693) by the Sacred Congregation for the Propagation of the Faith.

Often the Christian Hebraists were helped by rabbis or converts, but sometimes they heroically confronted the rabbinic corpus alone, doubtless making egregious errors, but in solitude producing monumental works of interpretation that, in the prearchaeological world and in a primitive period of Oriental philology, transmitted rabbinic thought to Christian divines, litterateurs, and even ordinary middle-class readers possessed by a desire to learn about the ancient religion of the Jews.

There was no consensus among the seventeenth-century Christian Hebraists about what worth they should bestow upon the interpretations of the Talmudists and rabbinic commentators. But they were generally prepared to consult them, to learn Hebrew and less frequently Aramaic, and to accept their descriptions of the rites of the Hebrews at the time of Christ as indications of the Lord's meaning in difficult passages of the Scriptures. There was a general presumption that Judaism had been frozen for sixteen centuries and that the evidence presented by contemporary Jews and their writings was a fairly accurate reflection of belief and practice among the ancient Hebrews. If few would credit Lightfoot's long lists of parallel passages in the New Testament and in the Talmud,[4] and if others like Jacques Basnage saw no reason to appreciate a rabbi's explication of the Bible more than a Christian divine's, there was rarely a scholar who would deny that he had profited to some extent from the linguistic knowledge of the rabbis. The Christian scholars might feel that the rabbis multiplied distinctions excessively and exaggerated their capacity to deduce new laws and rules from brief texts in Scripture, but they could not reject them outright. Except for a minority of Christian mystagogues who were seduced by Christian Knorr von Rosenroth's potpourri, the *Kabbala Denudata* (1677, 1684), the Protestant sects of the post-Renaissance world were commonsensical and preferred to steer clear of the Cabbalists. And when in the eighteenth century the French Abbé Augustin Calmet published his Gargantuan twenty-two volume commentary on the Bible, he was careful to call it literal, to distinguish it from allegorical interpretations, which had gone out of fashion.[5]

Seventeenth- and early eighteenth-century Christian commentators frequently raised questions that involved matters of fact—the scientific and business spirit introducing mundane concerns into the realm of the sacred. Chorography, really sacred geography, was ordered, biblical chronology set aright, and sacred chronology inserted into a world chronology of ancient peoples in such a manner that no gentile nation might appear to have priority over Israel. But meticulous historicization in the long run led to desacralization.

The trickle of printed Latin translations from the rabbis in the fifteenth century—incunabula like the *Aphorismi* of Maimonides and Rashi's commentary—had by the eighteenth swelled to a steady flow. In the years 1698 to 1700, under the direction of Surrenhuis, there had appeared in Amsterdam three vast folios containing the whole of the Mishna in Hebrew, a parallel Latin translation, along with Latin versions of the commentary of Maimonides and of Rabbi Obadia of Bonitera. The splendidly printed work of Surrenhuis—which was in Voltaire's library, now in Leningrad[6]—is enlivened with engravings illustrating the performance of rituals by noble Hebrews in Oriental, that is, Turkish, costume, or depicting scenes that make vivid and realistic the intricate problems of Sabbath violations or the dietary laws. The postures of the Hebrew gentlemen resemble those of baroque saints, and the general impression conveyed is that of a civilized people with a highly developed legal system. The translator's introduction stresses the importance of the Mishna for understanding Saint Paul, the disciple of Rabbi Gamaliel—a stock justification for Hebraic studies—and dwells on the significance of Paul's legal training as an element in his skillful propagation of the faith in Christ among the Romans. Talmudic and rabbinic Judaism served pre-Enlightenment Christianity in its scholarly attempt to understand itself.

The *philosophes*-litterateurs of the Enlightenment first saw ancient Judaism through the heavy lenses of the Christian Hebraists. Whenever they found them too weighty in their original form, Pierre Bayle and Jean Le Clerc and Basnage, who spanned the two centuries and wrote in French, acted as guides or transmitters. The major French *philosophes* of the eighteenth century, educated before the expulsion of the Jesuits, read Latin fluently and did not always have to rely on *haute vulgarisation*. English Deists of the early eighteenth century who had gone to Oxford had available the Latin commentaries and treatises of their seventeenth-century countrymen, whose texts they translated with a certain license. Thus the Enlightenment thinkers disseminated notions of Judaism that rested on information culled from respectable seventeenth-century Christian Hebraists at first or second hand. What they did with the data effected a revolution in Christian Europe's perception of Judaism.

Many of the Christian Hebraist commentators had produced rather sympathetic accounts of the ancient Hebrews, even when peppered with derogatory asides about Judaic rites. Their studies of the chronology and the chorography of biblical literature, of surviving manuscript texts from all centuries, were intended to eradicate discrepancies among the variant versions so that the proof of prophecies might be accurately demonstrated. They found the coming of Jesus the Messiah foretold in hundreds of Old Testament verses. The Deists and *philosophes* of the next century took these writings, with their profuse citations from rabbinic sources, as evidence that the whole postbiblical Judaic inheritance was a confused mess, and they quickly exploded the relevance of the messianic proof texts. Christianity was being loosened from its Judaic moorings in one breath, while in the next, everything that was muddled, miraculous, or counterfeit in contemporary Christianity was tarred as a derivation from Judaism. In approaching the *philosophes'* attack on the God of the Jews, it would be futile to look for consistency. Just as nineteenth-century Jews were denounced as subversive revolutionary communists and pillars of international capitalism at the same time, in the eighteenth century Judaism was at once proclaimed the progenitor of an absurd and iniquitous Christianity and denied as having any true connection with so universal and spiritual a religion.

III

The brazen re-examination of reality by men of the Enlightenment—including their radical revaluation of Judaism and Christianity—was based upon a set of conceptions that they rarely doubted. It was assumed that the remote origins of a phenomenon or the early history of a collective body such as the Hebrews told what was most important about the thing itself. They thought it was possible to arrive at these origins by a procedure they often called unveiling. There was a Platonism unveiled, a Christianity unveiled, an antiquity unveiled, the human heart unveiled, nature unveiled. And to unveil Judaism was an undertaking of the same character. All collectives, like persons, had a quintessential core, an *esprit* that was their epitome. The idea is traceable to theories of humors and characteristics and psychologies that implied the existence of a dominant passion in individuals and in nations. Montesquieu's *Spirit of the Laws* and Herder's doctrine of the *Volksgeist* are examples of this conviction. The *esprit* of a nation or a religion was thought to be readily discoverable, definable, and identifiable in simple terms. It was held to be pervasive throughout the organism and relatively impervious to the ravages of time. In harmony with this presupposition, books on the *esprit* of various nations multiplied. In the twentieth century, the working out of the *esprit* of a religion or culture might become rather sophisticated in the hands of an anthropologist or a sociologist, but the fundamental conception has not changed much since the Enlightenment.

The French literary men of the eighteenth century, unlike the polymath philologists of the seventeenth, generally rendered pejorative judgments of ancient Judaism in terms that went far beyond a formal indictment of its principal theological beliefs. In the writings of one of the *patres majores* of the Enlightenment, Voltaire, aversion to Judaism assumed the proportions of an obsession, especially in the last fifteen years of his life. With the critical edition of the one hundred volumes of Voltaire's letters, it is possible to follow the constancy of his Judeophobia from a shadowy period of his life in the 1720s—when he was flirting with Cardinal Dubois, with espionage, with court Jews in Germany deeply involved in the munitions business and thus having access to state secrets—through his last years, when this indefatigable defender of the rights of Protestants and freethinkers against the Catholic Church would never use the word Jew without prefixing it with the adjective *execrable*. In a letter written toward the close of his life he burst out that a Jew was a man who should have engraved upon his forehead the words "fit to be hanged."[7]

Personal psychological explanations for Voltaire's fixation have been attempted since the eighteenth century, when it was first observed and his vituperative attacks on historical Judaism were answered by a learned French abbé posing as a spokesman for Polish, Portuguese, and German Jews.[8] The "cause" of his hatred has been found in his money quarrels and lawsuits with court Jews, bankers, and speculators, some of whom had worsted him in business dealings. Jewish historiographers have toyed with the question at least since Heinrich Hirsch Graetz, and many have related it to his crusade against all positive religions. By some diabolical prefiguration of future events, one of Voltaire's nicknames in his select circle of friends was "Goebbels."[9] One might half-seriously venture the idea that Voltaire found in Jews and ancient Judaism a fetish into which he could pour those aspects of his being that he loathed in himself. François-Marie Arouet, a mere notary's son on the make, who changed his name and became a rather sycophantic court Christian, hated the fawning court Jews who had also changed their names. One cannot read his circumstantial descriptions of massacres and buttocks-beatings in *Candide*, or note his obvious enjoyment in recounting how Phineas the Levite entered the tent of the Jew lying with a Midianite woman and pierced her belly and his private parts with one thrust of the spear, without being aware of the cruelty in the man, which expressed itself in his tirades against the cruelty of the Jews.

If personal psychological and socioeconomic motives are underplayed, left as a sort of grim obbligato, and the traditional Joshua-like bifurcation of Christians into Judeophobes and Judeophiles is avoided, there remains the broad question of the ways in which, on the overt level, the Enlightenment responded to ancient Judaism. Granted that the perception of ancient Judaism cannot be divorced from the realities of eighteenth-century Jewish life, the portraits of the God of the Jews that were drawn during this period survived the Enlightenment and became dynamic historic forces in their own right. This was the first encounter of secular European intellectuals (emancipated or quasi-emancipated from traditional Christian angels and devils) with ancient Judaism, and new cultural stereotypes were fashioned that have endured for centuries.

IV

To attack with violence the barbaric customs and punishments of the ancient Hebrews as they were profusely recorded in the Bible, to lay bare the treacheries and butcheries of the kings of Judea and Samaria, to expose the falsehood of pretensions to miraculous performances in violation of the laws of nature, was a primary mission of the *philosophes*. To neglect a commonsense evaluation of the sacred writings of the Jews would have violated the very motto of the Enlightenment, Kant's *Sapere aude*.

The Enlightenment witnessed the falling apart of that uneasy Renaissance syncretism between the inherited traditions of Christianity and pagan, Greco-Roman philosophical conceptions. In some quarters it also meant the disengagement from each other of the Jewish and the Christian inheritances, which had once been linked with the bonds of Scripture and inveterate mutual loathing. As long as the Jews were condemned to continue their miserable lives as an eternal witness to the horror of deicide, they were a part of the world order with a role to play. Their existence had at least a satanic meaning. If the prophetic proof texts of the Old Testament were miraculous demonstrations or prefigurations of the truth of Christianity, the Jews had deeper meaning, even if they refused to accept the plain evidence of their own messianic writings. But what if *philosophes* or Deists showed that the essential moral truths of Christianity were as old as Creation? What need was there then for Hebrews ancient or modern? The later English Deists hoped to transform the existing orthodox ecclesiastical establishments into a Christianity even more watery than Herbert of Cherbury's original five tenets of religion. In this so-to-speak third dispensation, there was neither room nor need for Judaism as a prolegomenon to Christianity. If one believed that Christianity was as old as the Creation—to adopt the title of a well-known

pamphlet by the Deist Matthew Tindal—Judaism had not fulfilled any special theological purpose in the past and was of no
worth in the present. It was in effect an outlandish example of the
heavy incrustation of man-made ceremonials and priestly impositions upon a pure and simple set of Deist principles. Since miracles were exposed as frauds and prophecies shown to be superstitions or errors, what was the point of studying the texts of the
Jewish prophets in order to prove the coming of Christ? The truths
of Deism were engraved in the heart and mind of every man and
the rout of ceremonials and dogmas about which men disputed
was so much arrant nonsense. Judaism had accumulated more
ritualistic prohibitions than other religions and was the more
ridiculous for it.

One branch of the Enlightenment made Judaism useless: It was
not necessary for a purified Christianity in Europe. The Jews lost
their place in a Christian divine order of things and they soon
stood as naked aliens in a secular society. To the extent that Deism
triumphed, it left Jews isolated, irrelevant, a sport in the history
of Christianity. They became a mere remnant of ancient barbaric
tribes, living on in the midst of civilized Europeans, preserving bizarre fanatical customs. Lessing is regarded as Judeophile in popular Jewish historiography, and his relations with Moses Mendelssohn are a touching record of friendship; but if one reads carefully
the hundred theses of Lessing's *Education of Mankind,* Judaism
is stage one, Christianity stage two, and the new Enlightenment
supersedes them both in a stadial succession.[10] Judaism has lost
its reason for further existence.

When Voltaire played the Deist, his weapons were cruder. His
underlying purpose—to attack Judaism and Christianity by con-
flating them—was plainly expressed in a letter of 1765 addressed
to the Count and Countess d'Argental. He was writing a commentary on his own *Philosophie de l'histoire,* which had appeared
pseudonymously as the work of the Abbé Bazin: "This book modestly shows that the Jews were one of the latest peoples to appear,
that they took from other nations all their myths and all their
customs. This dagger once dug in can kill the monster of super-

stition in the chambers of men of good will without the fools even knowing it."[11] On another occasion he had written: "It is good to know the Jews as they are and to see from what fathers the Christians are descended."[12]

Out of unheroic caution, which characterized many, though not all, the *philosophes,* the early history of the Church, the lives of Christ and the apostles, were considered off limits. Most of the *philosophes* were determined to illuminate mankind without being martyred by it, to adapt Beccaria's formula. As a result, the particular God of the Jews and His chosen people were often surrogates that the *philosophes* fashioned to their own purposes and then lashed.

Abbé Calmet's volumes of commentary provided the raw materials for Voltaire's biblical exegesis. Received as a prominent royal historiographer in Calmet's monastery, Voltaire stayed for almost a month in his workshop, and has left an amusing description of the monks scurrying up and down ladders to search out texts that ultimately fed Voltaire's bonfires of both traditional Christianity and Judaism. Beelzebub took the pious facts assembled by the monks and twisted them to fiendish purpose. But he also went to original sources. Even a cursory examination of the collection of Church Fathers in his library, which has been kept intact from Catherine the Great through Andropov, bears witness to the assiduousness with which Voltaire consulted the sacred writings of early Christianity. In the dense forests of patristic literature, he carefully set up his own markers, little dabs of thin paper pasted on passages that might some day be useful in the anticlerical crusade. He set out to prove that the Jews had a material and anthropomorphic image of God: He spoke, the Jews maintained, ergo He had an actual voice. Judaism was carnal. By adhering to the literal, factual meaning of the Bible, Voltaire rendered it inconsistent and contradictory, even repulsive. Reading in the Book of Joshua that the victorious war leader circumcised all Jews who had been born during the decades in the wilderness and had been wandering about uncircumcised, Voltaire conjured up the spectacle of a veritable mountain of foreskins on Gilgal.

What the Jews wrote was fiction and not to be believed. Then he turned about abruptly and uncritically accepted biblical statistics when they concerned the Hebrews on a slaughtering rampage of enemies and sinners, in order to illustrate the cruelty of the God of the Jews. To Isaac de Pinto of Amsterdam, who in a respectful letter had protested some of his remarks on the Jews, he wrote: "Remain a Jew since you are one, but don't massacre 42,000 men because they could not pronounce shibboleth right nor 24,000 because they slept with Midianites; be a *philosophe*. . . ."[13]

When literate freethinkers of the Enlightenment had to weigh the witness of the Old Testament on the nature of Judaism against the witness of their favorite Roman historian, Tacitus, in his famous excursion on the character of the Jews in Book 5 of the *Histories,* there could be no question that the scales would tilt heavily on the side of Tacitus. For them he was a true, objective, pagan historian, not involved in the quarrels of Christians and Jews. He was a contemporary, first-century, civilized Roman official, who had sifted the tales about the Jews, the origin of their religion, their exclusiveness, the contempt in which they were held by all nations, and the hatred they reciprocated. Tacitus' account of how Moses instituted new religious rites in order to bind to himself the tribes of Jews driven out by the Egyptians was consonant with prevalent eighteenth-century theories about the origin of Oriental religions: The religion was an invention of a leader or a priest and had no intrinsic meaning. The idiosyncratic idea of having an empty temple with no representation of the invisible god was for Tacitus a patent demonstration of Jewish absurdity. The Jews were contentious among themselves, but extraordinarily stubborn in clinging to their fatuous beliefs when the Romans attacked them. As a tribe in the Roman Empire, they were peculiar, obdurate, and troublesome, nothing more. Reading Tacitus, Enlightenment *philosophes* thought they recognized eighteenth-century Jews. One had to be wary of them.

If the most relevant part of the Old Testament for theorists of the political state in Christian society was the history of kingship, particularly its cloudy inception under Samuel, for the theologians who were apologists of Christianity, as well as for those who would crush the infamous beast or at least cut its fangs, the heart of the matter was the nature of prophecy in ancient Judaea. It was here that the English Deists and French *philosophes* exerted their major effort in pulling Judaism and Christianity apart.

Among orthodox believers, Christianity was proved both by the miracles that Christ performed, witnessed by apostles and the people, and by the evidence of what were considered the prophetic passages of the Old Testament, verses in which the coming of Christ the Messiah had been foretold. In orthodox Christian theology of the seventeenth and eighteenth centuries, there was a growing apologetic movement in one direction: Miracles were substantially underrated, especially in the non-Catholic world, and the main witness, proof, or demonstration of the truth of the Christian religion inexorably shifted to prophecy. Protestants regularly mocked ongoing Catholic miracles such as the periodic liquefaction of the blood of Saint Januarius in Naples. Locke and Newton, for whom miracles were a subject of some consequence during their frequent religious colloquies, had settled upon a compromise: Miracles had ceased after the first centuries of Christianity because thereafter further demonstrations of divine will in the natural order would have been excessive, supererogatory, a violation of the scientific law of parsimony. Rationalism, skepticism about the accuracy of the senses, made reports of miracles that had occurred thousands of years ago weak reeds to lean upon, since men of sound mind doubted even contemporary ones.

The written testimony of Old Testament prophets became the preferred battleground of both believers and unbelievers. In his customary manner, Holbach once "abridged" a work by Rabbi Isaac Balthazar Orobio de Castro and entitled it *Israel vengé;*[14] in this polemic Christian belief, which had found support in an interpretation of Isaiah 53 as foretelling the coming of Christ, was contradicted by a traditional Jewish reading of the text. Rabbinic Judaism was called to witness by Holbachian atheists to destroy prophecy as a persuasive demonstration of the truth of Christianity. As for the spirit of Judaism, the Holbachians took care of that in another context. The theological controversies over prophecy were a melee in which an observer from on high would often have had difficulty knowing on whose side the contenders were fighting. Did the proof texts of Isaiah and Haggai and Malachi refer to Christ or to some more immediate political events in the history of Judaea? Or were they prophecies about a future Messiah who was yet to come? Ingenious commentators like Jean Le Clerc, the remonstrant Genevan popularizer who ended up in Holland editing universal libraries for the learned, held that Old Testament prophecy might be at once a prediction of some immediate event, like the Jewish release from the Babylonian captivity, and a foretelling of a more distant Messiah. Ultimately Deist Christianity dispensed entirely with the philological refinements of rabbinic exegesis. Bereft of its primary function of prophesying the coming of Christ, the Old Testament lost much of its significance for Enlightenment Christianity.

What was an Old Testament prophet? Once Spinoza had answered the question in the *Tractatus Theologico-Politicus* (1670) in what appeared to many to be naturalistic terms, the character of the prophet became a key to the judgment of Judaism. Christians like the Anglican professor John Spencer, who had codified the writings of Maimonides in a Latin work, *De legibus Hebraeorum*,[15] adopted Maimonides' portrait of the prophet as a man learned, rational, of impeccable morals, probably rich, who, after having shown himself worthy of divine inspiration, established a special relationship with God. Enlightened Anglicans with Deistic leanings welcomed this portrayal of the prophet as a philosophical teacher, totally unlike the tinker prophets and ranters who had spoken with tongues during the English Civil War, a horde of wild, mad enthusiasts, lechers, ignoramuses, living among the dregs of society. Maimonides, the respectable Moses of Judaism, was a welcome philosopher to rationalist Anglican clergymen.

But the Maimonidean portrait of a prophet was soon besmirched. Voltaire and the members of Baron d'Holbach's atheist conventicle, perversely called the synagogue, drew a very different profile of a prophet. They read the biblical texts literally and spread the image of Amos the ignorant enthusiast, of Ezekiel running naked in the streets of Jerusalem. These prophets were blubbering lunatics who performed outlandish acts, married prostitutes. While orthodox believers took comfort in the wisdom of the prophets who had foretold the coming of Christ and sometimes naïvely talked of the "sons of the prophets" as sort of universities of ancient Judaea, those Deists who wanted neither Christ coming once or twice nor a future Jewish Messiah made the biblical prophets sound like the Protestant "prophets of London," those persecuted Huguenots from the Cévennes who were afflicted with glossolalia and held scandalous séances predicting doomsday. For the Enlightenment, Spinoza, whose works had been translated into the vernacular, had relativized prophecy and divine inspiration. Prophecy had acquired a taxonomy: There were different types of prophets. Some heard voices, some had dreams. The Moses who saw God was the greatest, to be sure. But prophets were legislators of a particular people and their admonitions had no universal applicability.

This rationalist and relativist attitude toward prophecy diverted the argument from God's nature and intent to the nation of the Jews. A Maimonidean theologian like Isaac Newton had gone to great lengths to show the absolute conformity of all prophetic utterances, Judaic and Christian. For him the historic events of prophecy derived their unity from God Himself, who could harbor no contradiction. Later in the century ancient Judaic prophecies were still widely regarded as historic events, but for Voltaire and the Holbachians they had become either the delusions of madmen or the planned deceptions of priestcraft.

V

Montesquieu taught that every nation had an *esprit* particular to itself and the mainspring (*ressort*) of its whole being. For the Romans it was a warrior spirit; for the Phoenicians it was commercial; for the ancient Hebrews it was religious. This conception of the dominant passion in a nation was complemented by another anthropomorphic analogy—each nation experienced a stadial development that stamped a different *esprit* upon its life in each individual period. Vico's three ages in the *Scienza Nuova* preceded Herder's *Volksgeist*, but despite marked distinctions in the definition and diagnosis of the stages, the idea itself is one of the most common and persistent notions of eighteenth-century thought. Even skeptical *philosophes* like Diderot, Hume, and Voltaire, who were most reluctant to imprint a stadial pattern upon the bewildering chaos of historical experience, distinguished at least two historical states among all nations—a condition of barbarism and a state of civilization. In passing judgment upon the nation of the Hebrews and their God, the *philosophes* had to find a place for them somewhere in this implicit system. Was the ancient history of the Hebrew nation the account of a barbarous or of a civilized people? The books of the Bible were opened to reveal harrowing delineations of the Jews and their priests and kings. For many *philosophes*, a barbaric Judaean kingship and a fanatical priesthood fitted together.

Travel literature described customs and habits of strange peoples in all parts of the world, many of them atrocious and cruel; but the question of whether or not the peoples were civilized turned on whether they had a system of laws. In this respect, once the Israelites had settled on both sides of the Jordan and occupied half of the Eastern Mediterranean littoral, it was difficult for even the most rabid Judeophobes of the Enlightenment to deny them a measure of civility. Diderot, perhaps with one eye cocked on the royal censor, included a dithyramb on Moses the legislator in the *Encyclopédie*. But there were those like Voltaire who were intent upon likening the Jews to the early Picts and Celts of Europe and the primitive Greeks. The parallel sacrifices of Iphigenia and of Jephthah's daughter was the stereotyped example. They drew from the Bible the portrait of a barbaric, not a civilized, kingdom. David was their exemplar monarch of ancient Judaism.

In his *Histoire du Vieux et du Nouveau Testament* (1705), Basnage the Huguenot exile and preacher at Rotterdam, who wrote what were probably the most popular eighteenth-century source books of secular knowledge about Jews and Judaism, had dropped the more licentious episodes of King David's life or psychologized

his misconduct to the point where the story of his iniquities became a morality play about the dangers of giving free rein to the
passions. Holbach and Voltaire took the same biblical narratives
and presented them as a Tacitus or Suetonius might in writing
about an emperor of Rome. Both the kings of the Jews and their
God turned out to be grisly characters if measured by the standards of Paris salon society or the club life of David Hume's
London.

The French anticlericals reveled in shattering the image of
David. The orthodox apologists of David had celebrated the piety
of his Psalms; in *David, ou l'histoire de l'homme selon le coeur de
Dieu* (1768), the Holbach circle turned to the simple facts narrated
in the books of Samuel and Kings. In the previous century, Rem-
brandt in a famous painting had drawn King David as a resplen-
dent Oriental monarch, repentant, deep in thought, listening to
the admonishments of an emaciated Nathan. For the Holbachians,
David the murderous lecher who had Bathsheba's husband Uriah
killed at the front and David the disloyal harpist made more plausible portraits. They pictured David as the head of a gang of ruf-
fians and his God as a capricious creature who poured ointment
about rather promiscuously. Pierre Bayle's article on David in the
first edition of the *Philosophical and Critical Dictionary* had
aroused such opposition that he was forced in the second edition
to suppress many of his acidulous comments; but they were later
restored, and the *philosophes* had regular recourse to him. The
brutal hacking up of King Agag by Samuel as graphically depicted
in Voltaire's play *David* may tell something about the dynamics
of Voltaire's personality; but whatever their motivation, Voltaire's
Old Testament scenes had a convincing goriness that the most
persuasive rabbinic apologies could not dispel. Not everything
written in the Enlightenment about the first dispensation was false
or even malicious in the light of a plain, straightforward reading
of the Bible.

Comparison of ancient Hebrew rites with the religious practices
of pagan neighboring nations revealed the polytheistic and idolatrous character of ceremonials described in the Bible, and dimin-

ished the reverence for Judaism as the first monotheistic religion. The *philosophes* quoted from the inflated volumes of Bishop Warburton's *The Divine Legation of Moses Demonstrated* (1742), which in a crude fashion propounded the thesis that the immortality of the soul was a conception introduced into Judaism only after the Babylonian captivity and denied the very idea of a world to come among the ancient Hebrews. That the ancient Jews did not believe in the soul's immortality became a historico-religious dogma and fed the timeworn notion that Judaism in its origins was carnal, dependent upon rewards in this world that were concrete, objective, and visible. It was but a step from there to the accusation that the Jews' absorption with accumulating money was derivative from their religion and inextricably bound up with it—the worship of Mammon. While the carnal temper was often attributed to the absurd multiplication of rabbinic interpretations, an early tendency was discerned in the laws of Leviticus and Deuteronomy themselves.

On a more elevated plane David Hume jumped to the conclusion that unphilosophical monotheism, by which he meant both institutional Christianity and Judaism, was incapable of holding to its lofty, abstract tenets and inevitably lapsed into the worship of objects and idols, and into the fear of hell reified as a place full of pitchfork-wielding devils.[16]

VI

In the clandestine publications of the Baron d'Holbach one is confronted with frank, militant, blatant atheism. There was nothing in Christianity, Deist or positive, that he wished to preserve. As a consequence, in describing the relationship of Judaism and Christianity, he argued that Christianity was simply reformed Judaism—and not much reformed at that. Voltaire and d'Alembert shuddered at the prospect of atheism when they read Holbach's writings, and scribbled "dangerous work" on the flyleaves. Jefferson, who studied all three of them, vacillated, as his marginalia show.[17] What Voltaire and d'Alembert feared were *dixsous* popularizations of Holbach's ideas that might corrupt the populace and lead to anarchy. Holbach, secure in his belief that society was protected by the hangman, not by God, let loose all the stops. The Holbachians assimilated Judaism to other primitive religions, generated and maintained by fear and terror. And fear, they had learned from the ancients, obfuscated truth and bred cruelty. The analysis of fear in primitive religion was pivotal in the attack on Judaism by Holbach and the engineer Nicolas-Antoine Boulanger, who frequented his salon. The fear of God in Judaism, the *Gottesfurcht* of sixteenth-century Lutherans, the highest virtue in a man, became identified with cruelty in eighteenth-century associationist psychology. And if the diverse branches of the Enlightenment were united in denouncing any single evil, it was cruelty.

The Holbachians reached the climax of their diatribes against the God of the Jews in *L'Esprit du Judaïsme, ou examen raisonné de la loi de Moyse, & de son influence sur la Religion Chrétienne* (1770), a work often imputed to the Deist Anthony Collins. Actually, it is a composite in which one can recognize the rhetoric of Boulanger, Diderot, and Holbach. The twelfth chapter, "The Influence of Judaism on the Christian Religion," is an oratorical display in which the parallel between the God of Christianity and the God of Judaism is set forth with a passion rarely attained in anticlerical literature even by Voltaire and Nietzsche. The full force of the battering ram is directed at the God of the Jews, of whom the Christian God is a mere replica.

Christians, like Jews, worship a cruel and gory God; they proclaimed one who demands blood to appease his fury. But is not cruelty a sign of weakness? Did God create his creatures in order to spill their blood? Nevertheless these abominable principles have been invoked to justify the atrocious persecutions that Christians have launched a thousand times against those whom they falsely imagined were the enemies of their God. Having made of this God a veritable cannibal, they have honored Him by avenging his cause with the fumes of human blood. It is in accord with these atrocious ideas that they imagined this same God demanded of the patriarch Abraham the blood of his only son and then demanded that to redeem men, the blood of a God, the blood of His own Son, be shed on the Cross.[18]

The Holbachians argued that in belief, in *esprit*, in ecclesiastical organization, the Jews were the very model of Christianity. Where orthodox Christians had seen the sacrifice of Isaac as a type for the Crucifixion, the Holbachians saw it as a despicable Oriental precedent that was imitated:

Blinded by their legislator the Jews never had any sound ideas of divinity. Moses devised an image for them with the characteristics of a jealous tyrant, restless and insidious, who was never restrained by the laws of justice and who owes nothing to men, who chooses and rejects according to his caprice, who punishes children for the crimes, or rather the misfortunes, of their fathers. . . . What more was needed to make of the Hebrew people a troop of slaves, proud of the favor of their celestial Sultan, prepared to undertake anything without examination to satisfy his passions and unjust decrees. This ignorant, savage people, imbued with the idea that its God was amenable to gifts, believed that it was enough to please Him to make Him many offerings, to placate Him with sacrifices, to enrich his ministers, to work in order to keep them in splendor, to fulfill scrupulously the rites that their cupidity dreamed up. . . .
These are the horrible features with which the legislator of the Hebrews painted the God that the Christians have since taken over.[19]

In this portrait, the God of love and mercy was completely stricken out.

Explaining the burning of marranos in contemporary Spanish and Portuguese autos-da-fé, the Holbachians returned Christianity to its origins—Judaism. It was as if the Jews had willed their own eventual destruction. "In a word, all the ferocity of the Judaic priesthood seems to have passed into the heart of the Christian priesthood, which since it has established itself on earth has caused barbarities to be committed unknown to humans before."[20]

VII

The last important Enlightenment interpretation of the spirit of Judaism was made not by the enemies of religion but by a group of Christian believers. It ended in emotionalizing and romanticizing the religion of Judaism as it was embodied in the Old Testament. This novel religious conception assumed two kindred forms in France and Germany: the romantic religiosity of the Vicar of Savoy's confession of faith in Rousseau's *Emile,* and the exaltation by Herder of the primitive Hebrew poetry of the Bible as the most sublime expression of the religious spirit.[21] Together they generated a religion of feeling that was related to moral beauty, and ultimately deflected traditional Western religions from their doctrinal and historical pathways—in some instances a departure so radical that the whole nature of religious experience underwent a profound change.

The effect on the view of Judaism was strongest in the German world, where Jewish communities were more numerous than anywhere else in Western Europe. In 1753 the Oxford professor of poetry Robert Lowth, later Bishop of London, whose Hebrew was in fact rather weak, had published his lectures *De sacra poesi Hebraeorum.* The German Hebraist Johann David Michaelis corrected his errors and perfected his reading of much of the Bible as poetry. Their discovery of the sacred poetry of the Hebrews was harmonious with Herder's definition of the core of ancient Judaism as its poetic nature. The essential spirit of Judaism had been made manifest in the earliest documents of the human race, the Scriptures. Language revealed the secret soul of every religious people, and the poetry of the Bible was the *Geist* of the ancient Hebrews in their very beginnings, their creative moment. Among the Hebrews early poetic language was the vehicle for the most sublime religious feeling. The rationalist theologies of all religions were secondary; it was the poetic language of religion in music and in verse that was closest to the divine. When Herder, while remaining a Lutheran, abandoned discussion of Jewish or Christian theology and identified the religion of Judaism with the beauties of the Hebrew language, he freed the spirit of Judaism from the contempt of the Voltaireans and the Holbachians. But at the same time he opened the way to aestheticizing religious experience among all peoples, which subtly robbed the Judaic dispensation of its uniqueness.

One aspect of Moses Mendelssohn's defense of Judaism was

deeply colored by a perception that he shared with his friends Michaelis and Herder. In aestheticizing the religion of the Old Testament, Christians and Jews could have a common experience. They could read Psalms and prophetic works, Mendelssohn wrote Michaelis, as poetry, without theological glosses and debates over whether or not they foretold the coming of a Messiah. They could ignore the exegetical apparatus that discovered prefigurations of Jesus in what were poetic effusions of the Judaic religious soul.[22] In his book *Jerusalem*, Mendelssohn likened religions to different languages in which the same universal humanity found a voice.[23] Though he continued to observe Jewish rituals meticulously, he appeared no longer to hold to their absolute religious importance, regarding them as man-made, like commentaries on texts or theological deductions. It was then that the Swiss pastor Johann Kaspar Lavater summoned him to become a Christian—an invitation that Mendelssohn rejected with angry vehemence. Since the moral truths of Judaism were the same as those of natural religion without revelation, since each religion was a divinely inspired language, why should he forsake the religion into which he had been born? Proselytization was presumptuous and conversion idiotic.

The consequences of this romantic, emotional transformation of Judaism into a religion of moral beauty were far graver than Mendelssohn imagined. The reduction of Judaism to an aesthetic-moral experience inflicted a more serious wound on traditional Judaism in the Germanic world than the sneering of a Voltaire intent upon its uglification. If Judaism and Christianity were equally appealing to the romantic imagination, why hesitate at the baptismal font? The convert Dorothea Schlegel, née Mendelssohn, was the visible outgrowth of this movement. The *raison d'être* for Judaism was being shattered by the celebration of the ancient God of the Jews as an inspirer of sweet and lofty poesy.

Despite his Judeophobia, Voltaire, too, was an admirer of the Old Testament as literature. He thought its dramatic incidents more gripping and vivid than those of the Homeric epics. Of course, like Shakespeare, the Bible violated the canons of good taste, and one spurned its wild coarseness in an enlightened age.

The Bible was an incarnation of the barbaric spirit and vigor of antiquity, not a model for civilized Europeans.

Thus, after the rupture of the traditional union of Christianity and Judaism, in which Judaism had played the stock role of a prolegomenon to the dominant European religious culture, there were at least three principal positions on Israel assumed in the Enlightenment. Some thinkers maintained that the essence of a spiritualized Christianity was universal from the beginning of time and they eliminated Judaism as a forebear. Others maximized the importance of Judaism, but saw it as the archetypal fanatical religion of which Christianity was a descendant, and piled up the evidence that it was unfit for any but barbarian peoples; the time had come for both Judaism and Christianity to be superseded by reason alone. Still others emotionalized or aestheticized religion, allowing for the appreciation on an equal plane of all religious languages, and the traditional belief in the Covenant between God and His chosen people evaporated.

VIII

Edward Gibbon once said of the religions of the Roman Empire that the mass of the people considered all the religions of the empire as equally true and that the magistrates believed them all to be equally useful. This may apply well enough to much of present-day American society. Gibbon also remarked that philosophers thought all religions equally false.[24]

In the two hundred years since the triumph of the Enlightenment, the religious temper of Western society has changed more radically than in any period since the birth of Christianity. Present-day Christian views of Judaism would be incomprehensible to the heads of the established eighteenth-century churches and to the theologians whose doctrinal positions have been outlined early in this essay. The pattern of distribution of Jews in the world has been dramatically altered. The Jewish inhabitants of Central and Eastern Europe have been wiped out; France has more than ten times as many Jews as it did in the eighteenth century; and North American Jews have become preponderant in the Diaspora. Christian belief has ceased to rest primarily upon miracles or proof texts of Old Testament prophecy. Conversion of the Jews is not a major preoccupation of any Christian denomination. The acerbity of speech of many Deists and *philosophes* has generally been left behind.

Christian giants of scholarship no longer devote themselves to Hebraism. Nevertheless, the world-wide flowering of biblical studies among Christians and Jews (stimulated in part by the discovery of the Dead Sea scrolls) has bestowed a new dignity on ancient Judaism as a religion. Israeli bibliolatry has not brought about the neglect of the rabbinic learning of postexilic Judaism, and the multifarious forms of historical Judaism are alive in Israel. Hebraic studies flourish in Jewish theological centers in America and in secular universities. Judaism as a historical religion is now rarely treated pejoratively.

In Vatican II, the Catholic Church denied the collective responsibility of Jews in all ages for the Crucifixion. Though many American Fathers of the Council had favored an explicit rejection of the "infamous blasphemy" of deicide, the final text fell short of this demand.[25] Nevertheless, a call was issued in the 1965 declaration *Nostra aetate* for the opening of a fraternal dialogue between Christians and Jews, whose common spiritual patrimony "is so great."[26] Doctrinal reconstructions are evident in deeds as well as in words—Catholic priests have made forthright avowals of *mea culpa*. The gospel according to John cannot be amended and teachings in some seminaries may perpetuate old ways of thinking; Jewish synagogues and cemeteries are the targets of aberrant manifestations of Judeophobia as they have been through the ages. But the degree to which residual hatred of Jews draws sustenance from Christian theology has diminished. Contemporary Judeophobia has roots in racial and economic doctrines that are far removed both from the traditional arguments of the Church Fathers and from the caricatures of radical atheists of the Enlightenment.

Protestants, loosely organized in a world council of churches, present a broad spectrum of attitudes toward Judaism, a few of which can be traced back to their eighteenth-century origins. There are Jews who feel that some Protestant sects have lagged behind the Catholic Church in their inner reformation with respect to Judaism, that the venom of Luther's Judeophobia has only been diluted. Understandably, Protestant fundamentalists and believers in biblical inerrancy are more involved with the Old Testament texts than are other sects, often with paradoxical consequences. The return of the Jews to the Holy Land enjoys the active support of many biblical literalists and millenarians, for whom the ingathering of Israel presages a fulfillment of prophecy. But at the same time they have questioned whether a Jew who does not recognize Christ can be saved. On occasion the whole ecumenical position recently adopted in Christian churches has been muddied by the parochial contention that God does not listen to the prayers of a Jew.

On the commonsense level, the forms and substance of Christian and Jewish religious life in America resemble each other. All Western Christian denominations have undergone the influence of eighteenth-century emotional revivalism. Romantic effusiveness in religion is on the rise and in this sense Western Christianity and Judaism have been associated in a common religio-aesthetic experience. The universal romantic religiosity of Rousseau—with more than a touch of nature worship—and the pietism of Herder and the expressive evangelical spirit of John Wesley have been victorious over the philosophical rationalism of Leibniz's conception of an ecumenical religion for all mankind. Jews who are neither Cabbalists nor Hassidim but belong to one of the three principal Jewish denominations in America—Orthodox, Conservative, and Reform—nevertheless draw the same kind of emotional sustenance from dalliance with the quasi-mystical Jewish sects. There are signs of increased religious observance among members of the three Jewish denominations, but the nature of their religious experience and their intensity of devotion are as varied as among their Christian neighbors. Memorable discourse on religious thought and feeling among Jews in twentieth-century America is rare, as it is among their Christian compatriots.

Ecumenicalism has been so pervasive that a Catholic church stripped of images looks much like a Protestant meeting house, and a Jewish sermon focused on current events is hardly to be differentiated from its liberal Protestant counterpart. Centuries-old Judaic moral admonitions to pursue justice and righteousness make it easy for a Jew to assimilate the social gospel of liberal Christianity; both religions at times seem to be turning into a kind of eighteenth-century Deism shorn of anticlerical polemics. The hyphenated adjective "Judeo-Christian," which was not in common usage in the Christian world before the twentieth century, has come to symbolize shared moral values. This idea would have been preposterous to apologists who wove theological systems around the contrast between Jewish carnality and Christian spirituality. In North America, having some religion is still a social, if not a political requirement for election to office, but fewer Americans care which religion is professed. Jews need not subject themselves to the humiliation of a conversion to Christ without conviction, as they did in nineteenth-century Germany. Religious pluralism in American society is taken for granted even more than ethnic diversity. It was a stereotype of eighteenth-century thought that religious intolerance was proportionate to zealotry and fanaticism, and that conversely nations like the Roman, rather indifferent in matters of religion, tended to be tolerant of the religious practices of others. If universal religious toleration was one of the wished-for human conditions in the Enlightenment, it has been largely realized in late twentieth-century America.

Since World War II there has been one development in Judaism that is momentous. Messianism and the longing for the return to Israel have been potent forces in traditional Judaism, though the eighteenth century was probably a low point in the history of this sentiment. In our time the existence of Israel as a state has been invested with religious meaning for a great number of Jews. Judaism, fervid or lukewarm, has been politicized. Reform Judaism of the nineteenth and early twentieth centuries, derived from Moses Mendelssohn, was long inimical to the commingling of religion and politics, and insisted on their complete separation, lest Jews be considered less patriotic than their fellow nationals in the lands where they lived. Today Reform Jews, once militantly hostile to Woodrow Wilson's approval of the Balfour Declaration, have joined Conservative Jews, Orthodox Jews, and other sects (except for tiny Jewish fundamentalist minorities that deny recognition to the state of Israel as a usurper of the Messiah's prerogatives) in moving the preservation of Israel as a political entity to a central position in their religious life. The prayer book of Orthodox Jews now includes a long text, promulgated by the chief rabbis of Israel, beginning: "Our Father who art in heaven, Protector and Redeemer of Israel, bless thou the State of Israel which marks the beginning of the flowering of our redemption." The careful phrasing still allows for the persistence of the traditional expectation of the coming of the Messiah at a future time. Conservative Jews have a briefer version that starts in the same way. And even Reform Jews, who in the nineteenth century eliminated from their devotions all references to Jerusalem and the resurrection of the dead, now pray for "the land of Israel and its people." This prayer for Israel is the only liturgical innovation on which the three Jewish religious divisions in America are in accord.

It may be difficult for Christians to comprehend the internal religious squabbles among Jews, to realize that there is no pope in Judaism, no world body that can speak for religious or secular Jews, no canonical law universally recognized by Jews. There is in fact great freedom in North America for any Jew to speak his mind on the orientation of the numerous religious synods and Jewish organizations of laymen that vie for his allegiance, or on the state of Israel and any of its wise, courageous, or foolhardy decisions. The persecutions of this century, however, have made Jews hesitant to alienate themselves from the general will of their community, ill-defined as it may be. Divergent interests of rich or poor, old settlers or new immigrants, belief in a false Messiah like Sabbatai Zevi or disbelief, Zionism or anti-Zionism, in their day have torn Jewish communities apart, and there is fear of divisiveness. The survival of Israel is now the heart of spiritual existence among American Jews. Their religious institutions have been thrust into the maelstrom of American and Israeli party politics. But the needs of a beleaguered state like Israel may not always dovetail neatly with the requirements of an ancient religion like Judaism. And an Enlightenment prophet might hold that a second coming of the holocaust is not reserved for Jews alone.

6 THEODICY OF A PIETIST

Almost everything that Herder composed became part of a theodicy, a providential philosophical history. Some works are directly addressed to the subject: the brilliant, youthful sketch, full of ironies and ambiguities, entitled *Auch eine Philosophie der Geschichte zur Bildung der Menschheit* (*Still Another Philosophy of History on the Development of Mankind*), 1774; the provocative, prize-winning essay, *Ursachen des gesunknen Geschmacks bei den verschiedenen Völkern, da er geblühet* (*Causes of the Decline of Taste among Peoples Where It Once Flourished*), 1775; the masterpiece of his mature years, the *Ideen zur Philosophie der Geschichte der Menschheit* (*Reflections on the Philosophy of the History of Mankind*), 1784–91; and the amorphous *Briefe zu Beförderung der Humanität* (*Letters toward the Advancement of Humanity*), 1783–97, in which the ideas of a garrulous scholar are so diffuse that they often revert to an original chaos. But other writings, those on primitive poetry, mythology, the spirit of Judaism and of Christianity, the literary achievements of all nations, the origin of language, and aesthetics, and even the abortive attempt at a philosophical critique of his former professor Immanuel Kant, can be assimilated as mammoth footnotes to the major themes of his philosophy of history.

To submit to the canons of consistency and Aristotelian logic Herder's variant formulations in the thirty-three volumes of the classical Suphan edition of his works is a vain and futile effort.[1] Rudolf Haym, his most eminent biographer, in a two-volume book published in 1880 and 1885 that shows no signs of aging, compared the *Ideen* to a bush whose branches and twigs sprouting in wild profusion end up breaking one another.[2] If Herder could not hold to a set position even within a single work, stability should certainly not be expected in a body of writings that spans more than three decades. Herder has bequeathed historical models that are sometimes flagrantly contradictory. It is best to look at these variegated designs in his own spirit of the moment, as the ways in which he experienced history at different times in his long literary life. Though he cast his seed in strange wombs and has many descendants who refuse to recognize one another, there are elements in his world history that are remarkably constant. He was not without bombast. The Pietist fervor of his background was translated into all manner of secular artistic enthusiasms that shifted with his life history. But for all their changeability, his passions and antagonisms were psychologically of a piece, even if the critic who approaches Herder's writings as he might a tightly reasoned text of Immanuel Kant's may be driven to distraction. Herder was one of those who spoke with tongues, like Meister Eckhardt and Luther before him, Hamann his contemporary, and Nietzsche and Spengler after him. Such men are the despair of analytical Anglo-Saxon and French historians.

Most twentieth-century scholarly argumentation about the essence of Herder's thought—and the debates seem interminable—is analogous to a dispute about which brilliant flower in a luxuriant tropical garden is its most characteristic expression. Did his work advocate cultural nationalism for all peoples or was it merely a nativist reaction against contemporary frenchifiers of the German spirit? Was he a primitivist, a worshiper of folk culture, or the ideological bearer of the values of the German bourgeoisie in its formative stage? Was he an exponent of the Enlightenment concepts of Humanity and Reason, one of the educators of German liberalism, or was he still at heart an enthusiastic German Pietist and the propagator of irrationalism? Was he the father of a virulent form of aggressive nationalism in central and eastern Europe, a militant exponent of Germandom who can be attached to a long line culminating in the National Socialists? Was he the crucial figure in the modern historicist revolution? A philosophical eigh-teenth-century precursor of Darwin? A racist? With the exception of the last epithet, which unfortunately found its way into Colling-wood's *Idea of History* and was thus spread in the English-speak-ing world, Herder was all of these things—and more.

Herder not only gave status to the culture of primitives, winning the appreciation of explorers like Johann Georg Forster for his capacity to look at peoples from within instead of regarding them as mere objects to be converted or "civilized"; he also placed a new value on the earliest form of expression of all peoples, the mythic. Admittedly, such an outlook bears with it "reactionary" dangers, and Herder's work has merged with streams of thought that have been blatantly antiprogressionist in a political sense, racist, and existentialist to the point of entirely rejecting the ra-tional. But a thinker should not be held morally responsible be-fore some self-appointed Grand Judge for the subsequent fortune of his ideas. The history of Herder's thought is, after all, the his-tory of other men's thoughts about him.

Herder's capacity for *Einfühlung,* empathy, makes him sound dilettantish at his worst, but at his best a great interpreter of states of feeling in other historical epochs. It is no accident that when Michelet was introducing Vico into France, his colleague Edgar Quinet was performing the same service for Herder. In the roman-tic tradition Herder sought to express individuality, but he was not blind to universals. He and Vico stand together as ideal mas-ters for one kind of historian—the man who sees the particular impregnated with the universal, but still seeks to re-create the par-ticular in all its uniqueness. Herder could evoke the genius of both the living and the dead, of Goethe and of ancient Hebrew poetry—no mean achievement.

Herder became a German culture hero not only among liberals and reactionaries, who each saw merely one side of his face, but among all those who believed in cultural riches for their own sake, who reveled in a full larder of historical experiences, in the sheer joy of variety and the plenitude of things. If this makes him an ideological representative of bourgeois civilization, so be it. But

Herder's pretension to living through all states of being in all times and places, the expansive ideal for which he stands, is, one must now admit, less ecumenical and all-inclusive than would have been imagined a generation ago. It is rather bookish, literary, primarily devoted to the corpus of Western aesthetic, philosophical, and religious expression, ornamented with a smattering of orientalia and reflections about primitives culled from the voluminous travel literature that he devoured.

Herder was a staid Lutheran pastor, who had served for years in Riga and in isolated Brückenburg. Born in 1744 in Mohrungen, the smallest town in the harsh wasteland of East Prussia, the son of an impoverished schoolteacher who had also discharged the duties of bellringer and cantor, Herder bore the mark of his origins. Though in 1769 he ventured on a journey to the West—to Paris, Holland, Hamburg—he always remained an outsider, a stranger among the sophisticated German courtiers who finally received him. He was not happy in his post as supervisor of educational institutions in Weimar. Goethe's affairs shocked him and so did European drunkenness, "immorality," and excess. One does not have to look hard for Herder's provincial, petty bourgeois prejudices. But, for all its limitations, his attempt to open wide the floodgates of historical experience among all peoples, great and small, who ever inhabited the globe, is grand, and his steadfast refusal to equate meaningful history with the history of states and empires is still a fighting doctrine, not the whipping of a dead horse.

Many eighteenth-century thinkers who viewed world history philosophically felt a justifiable pride in the achievements of the European civilization to which they belonged. They were not as alienated from their society as some recent commentators have fancied. They could contrast their own world of law with the barbarism of the Middle Ages. The *Encyclopédie* had revealed both to its writers and to its readers the wealth of knowledge that had been accumulated in all fields of human activity since the restoration of the arts and sciences; and if there were areas of the Continent where superstition and prejudice still cast a pall upon existence, the *philosophes* seemed to be steadily gaining ground, pouring illumination into the most dismal crannies of priestly dominion. Despite the persistence of religious and political persecution, even the skeptical among them saw themselves winning more battles than they were losing. If this was so, would they not go on from triumph to triumph developing the arts and sciences forever?

But here sober historical reflection gave some French and German thinkers pause. In France the political and aesthetic idea with which the intellectuals identified themselves was the age of Augustus and the Antonines; in Germany, the age of Pericles. These comparisons that inflated their pride also worried them as historians. We have observed Edward Gibbon wrestling simultaneously with the decline and fall of the Roman Empire and the symptoms of disease in the British dominion. The Roman Empire began to collapse precisely at the moment of its greatest extension. Was this to be the destiny of glorious eighteenth-century civilization? Would its institutions of order and civility give way before a new barbarian invasion, or would some deep-rooted malady sap the strength of a robust and thriving world? All the historical examples French and German thinkers could muster pointed to the pessimistic conclusion that in fact the most magnificent creations of mankind had fallen into ruins. There was no empire, however powerful, that had not declined, no age of flowering genius that had not been followed by a long period of aridity. How could enlightened Europe escape the destiny that had overwhelmed all other societies? Many eighteenth-century philosophical historians foresaw the demise of their own civilization. Death was natural and inevitable. Decay was the inescapable aftermath of growth and maturity. Studying past empires and the course of the ills that afflicted them, however, might still serve a salutary end: to find ways of prolonging the life-span of European civilization. Though death could not be avoided, the doctor of societies might at least stave off the doom as long as possible. A man did not disdain the advice of a wise physician merely because he knew he could not live forever.

Widespread as was this attitude, another direction of thought was emerging in France that bypassed those who brooded on the transitory nature of human institutions. For Turgot and Condorcet the Enlightenment was the great divide. The spell had been broken and new forces set in motion that would allow mankind to enjoy an eternally blooming state of civilization without interludes of barbarism. Men of the future would be born into a civilization, mature and creative, that would last forever. For those possessed with this spirit of optimism, analysis of the past would yield an answer to a vital question: What was there so essentially different in the character of present-day society that allowed it to achieve immortality? What corrosive evils of the past had been and would be eradicated? The burden of proof was upon the philosophical newcomers who made bold to imagine an unprecedented, unnatural fate, infinite progress for contemporary society. The usual response in France pointed to the development of the sciences, which, it was believed, had attained so great a momentum that it could never decelerate. A rather sophisticated theory of inevitable and infinite perfectibility embracing ever wider areas of the globe reached its epitome in Condorcet's *Esquisse*.

Although there were some supporters of this French thesis on the eastern side of the Rhine, writers in Germany with deeply religious roots in a dark Protestant view of human destiny could not accept the facile French idea of the cosmopolitan, unitary progression of the human mind, the inevitable elimination of decay and death. Herder, the outstanding representative of a new religious German philosophical history that diverged from the French current of linear, rationalist progression, altered the traditional historical perspective and the universe of historical discourse in a revolutionary manner. He conceived the history of mankind as a development not only of the human mind, the parochial French view, but also of the multifarious expressions of human nature beyond the rational. Shifting his emphasis from the history of individual polities, however great, to the whole world history of mankind, Herder argued that the life cycles of particular states had to end in death, but that in the plenitude of God's creation there was an infinite succession of individual cultures constantly being brought forth. Herder's interpretation of God's overall design in the governance of the world is as epoch-making as his discovery of a new historical consciousness.

How could it be, Herder asked rhetorically in the preface to his *Reflections on the Philosophy of the History of Mankind,* that the history of men on earth, unlike any natural history or series of events which had ever been contemplated, should not admit of a design? "Shall . . . God depart from his wisdom and goodness in the general destination and disposition of our species, and act in these without a plan?"[3] The recourse of some religious thinkers to the argument that God had decided to keep hidden the design of the history of mankind was evasive. It was contrary to reason to believe that He would reveal to man so many secrets of the "inferior part of creation" in the chain of being, the mysteries of the life of lower animals and of inanimate nature, and then draw a veil over the plan of mankind's history.

Herder, the religious Protestant clergyman brought up on the Old Testament, was reluctant to fly directly in the face of the Book of Job, which questions man's right to inquire into the rule of God on earth. And yet Herder cannot ignore the human need for a vision that extends beyond the petty sphere of daily activity. "[F]or where is the man, who discerns only the little purpose of his own life?"[4] To leave men without any understanding of the providential design would undermine faith. When men perceive nothing of the divine plan, they wonder whether there is one at all, and general religious incredulity spreads. Though they may fervently wish to believe in a plan, they are obliged constantly to stifle their misgivings as they regard the terrors and tragedies of life around them.

They constrain themselves not to consider the human race as a nest of emmets, where the foot of a stranger, himself but a large emmet, crushes thousands, annihilates thousands in the midst of their little great undertakings, where lastly the two grand tyrants of the Earth, Time and Chance, sweep away the whole nest, destroying every trace of it's existence, and leaving the empty place for some other industrious community, to be obliterated hereafter in it's turn. Proud man refuses to contemplate his species as such vermin of the Earth, as a prey of all-destroying corruption: yet do not history and experience force this image upon his mind? . . . Is not Time ordained as well as Space? Are they not the twin offspring of one ruling power?

To accept the idea that Space is full of wisdom, as Newton demonstrated, and that Time is full of disorder, is preposterous. Man is evidently formed to seek after order, to look beyond a point of time, and to build upon the past, for which reason he is provided with memory and reflection. But then again,

. . . does not this building of one age upon another render the whole of our species a deformed gigantic edifice, where one pulls down what another builds up, where what never should have been erected is left standing, and where in the course of time all becomes one heap of ruins, under which timid mortals dwell with a confidence proportionate to it's fragility?[5]

In this passage Herder was openly wrestling with his own doubts before his readers. As he surveys the cruel chaos of history his religious anguish approaches the despair of a believer wavering in his faith in God. To question meaning, plan, or design in history was almost equivalent to questioning the existence of God. Herder's introduction makes his philosophy of history a branch of apologetics. Having uttered, and in a way exorcised, his terrible apprehensions Herder abruptly abandons his painful thoughts. "I will pursue no farther this chain of doubts, and the contradiction of man with himself, with his fellows, and with all the rest of the creation: suffice it, that I have sought for *a philosophy of history* wherever I could seek it."[6]

In Herder's new philosophical view there was a single humanity with a history, despite the more immediate and arresting observation that the world was an agglomerate of widely dispersed and differentiated peoples and cultures, with a bewildering variety of languages, beliefs, and customs. Here a musical analogy came to his rescue. Every one of the infinite variations on the theme of man had an autonomous existence; but as each came into being and was fulfilled in time, total humanity *sub specie aeternitatis* was enriched. In the course of history all possible combinations of human sensibility, the form-giving elements in the varieties of experience, would make their appearance. There was no absolute historical death for mankind, because every culture that had been or would be fashioned, from the worm-eating Californian tribe through the Greek, became a part of one world symphony with an ever grander orchestration. At a later period Hegel made this conception more rationalist and restrictive by envisaging a limited number of embodiments of World-Spirit, defined primarily in terms of subject-object relationships, and by tracing them in simple sequence chronologically and geographically from East to West, from ancient despotic China to nineteenth-century Germany. Herder had allowed for no such formal chronological or geographic arrangement. Despite the semblance of historical sequence in which his cultures are introduced in parts of the *Ideen,* their filiations are tenuous. The cultural manifestations of the human are myriad, unpredictable, and discontinuous.

The style of living in the German Hanseatic cities and principalities where Herder spent many years was a shallow imitation of the French court, and his whole creative intellectual vision may be looked upon as a rejection of this artificially imposed way of life, with its emphasis upon the progress of arts, sciences, and civility, described in neat French categories. The French way was viewed simplistically by foreign eyes as a monolith to be accepted or rejected in its entirety. The "rationalism" and generalizing quality of French thought that Herder denounced were straw men of his own making. In his treatment, the French love of mathematical abstraction, which became the butt of his caustic irony, was primarily a foil for his own way of looking at the world. His organismic sense, his romantic holism, his demand that the perception of experience be unmathematical, concrete, colorful, more varied and emotive, less rigid and uniform, his denial of the traditional body-soul, reason-emotion dichotomy, was a counterattack of great magnitude launched from the East. Feeling was knowledge of an order superior to French reason, he argued.

Herder took pains to distinguish his universal history from the canonical French study of the eighteenth century, Montesquieu's *Spirit of the Laws,* even though he had derived from it the insight that climate affected the spirit of nations. He quickly set himself in opposition to the Frenchman's use of the generalization. He saw Montesquieu as making false abstractions from existential reality and the complexity of history when he set up the categorization of three types of states, monarchical, aristocratic, and democratic. No state form could be identically repeated in a different part of the globe even though it might bear the same name. Montesquieu had described states in terms of their professed constitutional principles, what they said they were; Herder knew that "verbal principles" of governments had little relationship to actual practice, performance, or existence. Montesquieu had taken his constitutional examples out of context, making them timeless, spaceless, and characterless. For Herder peoples had existed and grown only in these three dimensions. True philosophical history would have to be deeply rooted in the peculiarities of time, place, and national character as essential elements. Philosophical generality would follow these three forces through the details of *Volk* history. The result would be the authentic living, colorful pageant of the interplay of the three variables. The cyclical principle of the unfolding of history would always be the same, the separate *Volk* experience always different.

Herder's idea of a *Volk,* which I freely translate as nation or people, would dismay modern analytic philosophers like Frege, who stalwartly insists that "a concept that is not sharply defined is wrongly termed a concept." For myself, the fluidity of the idea is the primary guarantee of its vitality. Herder's usage is characteristically loose. The term *Volk* embraces the chosen people of Israel, the Greeks, the Egyptians, the Romans, the Germans, as well as tiny tribes of American Indians and Negroes in the African bush. A *Volk* is virtually any group that has a name and a culture. If there is a mythology, a poetry, a separate religion, a cuisine, a recognizably different pattern of sense perceptions, the *Volk* is identifiable. Herder's definition also applies to peoples that have no artifacts, or hardly any, and little mythology. There is, however, no folk without a religion, he affirms in deliberate denial of Bayle's and Hume's assertions, based on their reading of travel reports, that nations of atheists existed.

I

There are in Herder subtle attempts to relate the individual, the *Volk,* and Humanity as three organisms that grow in accordance with an inner genetic principle. Their interrelationship is one of the most difficult conceptions for him to expound, and he sometimes covers over the inadequacy of his presentation with mere rhetoric and effusive language. The analogy between the individual and his *Volk* is most convincingly elucidated, for both have life cycles, particular characters and spirits, and both are subject to accident, premature death, or corruption by alien influences. The individual cannot express himself in universal terms, for however extraordinary his genius he is bound by the realities of space, the original spirit of the *Volk* into which he was born, and the character of the time in the life history of his people. It is impossible to imagine his transcending these geographic and temporal circumstances, for he cannot define himself except in terms of a particular religion and in a specific language, a feeling pattern of images instilled into his soul through traditions transmitted and kept alive in myth, folk songs, religious ritual, and speech. These are not limitations in any mechanical sense, but rather expressions of differentiated character that excludes from being all other things except itself. When Herder evoked the creations of a man—and he wrote vivid appreciations of the major figures of world literature—he considered them as voices of the *Volk* spirit as well as of the author's own nature. If a poet tried to assimilate what was not his natural *Volk* spirit he would never be able to give utterance to a harmonious song; its bastard quality would obtrude.

The connection between a particular *Volk* and Humanity is cloudier, though in a sense Humanity is to the *Volk* as the *Volk* is to the individual. Humanity too has a growth, but it appears to be everlasting and knows no death. In the course of its development, its progression through time, numerous individual *Völker* are born, mature, and die, while Humanity lives eternal. There is no necessary transmission of the creations of one *Volk* to another, and even when contact is made through war or commerce, spiritual interpenetration rarely takes place because the outer shell of a *Volk* spirit is hard, virtually impenetrable. Thus there is no progress in the mechanistic or arithmetic sense in which some of the French *philosophes* used the term. *Völker* have fundamental attributes that are universal: a religion, art, a form of reason, and a morality. In this respect there is one Humanity. The *Völker* in their natural state are neither bestial nor angelic but uniquely human, and a *Volk*—unless corrupted (this is the implicit caveat)—can express only human values and ideas. The progress of Humanity means the realization in time of all possible *Volk* configurations. These entities were not created simultaneously, for it was the divine purpose that they come into being as history gradually unfolded itself.

Herder also employs the term *Humanität* as an attribute, a natural inclination or propensity of all mankind, that must be fostered and developed in each *Volk*, or it will be stunted.[7] It has manifested itself quintessentially not in the state and in the organization of power but in music, literature, art, and science, perhaps in that order of importance. The state as an embodiment of energy—*Kraft*—plays a dubious role. Herder is unalterably opposed to the aggressive Prussian kingdom of Frederick II; he is rarely favorable to the two Romes, the Roman Empire and the Holy Roman Empire; and he is no admirer of Louis XIV and his successors. The state is usually, though not always, described as a destructive force that crushes cultural flowers, amalgamates forms, stifles creative spirit. The modern European conquerors and colonizers of the world are depicted as ravishers of primitive peoples; the ancient Romans, praised for the virtues they displayed when they were a self-contained society living on their seven hills, were enemies of *Humanität* when they became imperial and extended themselves. The *Humanität* that Herder saw in all nations embodied eighteenth-century ideal values—Christian and Stoic—

without theology, sensate but not debauched, rational but not rationalistic, religious without clerical dogmatism.

But Herder was not wholly at ease with the history of separate cultures evolving in a biological rhythm. The universalist, French conception of progress confronted and challenged him. He struggled all his life with the postulates of the French progressionist school. At moments he mockingly dismissed those who applauded the development of the arts and sciences, their grand technological results—an increase in power—or their pleasure-enhancing gadgets. He drew upon a vast body of illustrations that equated luxury with effeminacy and moral degeneration. An increase in pleasure was no proof of any kind of superiority. Like most of his compatriots, Herder was still close to Rousseau's paradox in the *Discourse on the Arts and Sciences,* and he was an upright Pietist. The expansion of human technological power through invention was at best a half-good; in a telling passage of *Letters Toward the Advancement of Humanity* he asked whether the end to which this power was directed should not be a more central concern than its maximization.

On the other hand there are entire sections of his major work where in commonsense terms he viewed Western civilization— the chain from Greece and Rome through the present—as a unity, and concluded with a simple optimism that witnessed and celebrated the bourgeois virtues of orderliness, peace, diligence, workmanship. Herder praised the extension of the reign of law, the mitigation of cruel punishments. Even the medieval Papacy came in for a measure of niggardly approval as the institution that helped put an end to the wars of feudal nobles. No one outdid Herder in the zeal of his Protestant animosity against the Roman Catholic hierarchy; and yet he could concede in the last pages of the *Reflections* that perhaps this oppressive institution had served a purpose in binding together the barbarous peoples of the Middle Ages, who might otherwise have engaged in endless fratricidal wars and left Europe a Mongolian desolation. While hostile forces, spiritual and temporal, were subjecting the body of medieval

Europe to pressures and counterpressures, a third force arose, a good middle-class power with knowledge, utilitarian industriousness, and diligence, a force that ultimately prevailed and made it possible to dispense with both the warring knights and the obscurantist Papacy. True Europe emerged in a culture of business, science, and art which were translated into Reason and everstronger community relationships.

Herder sometimes approximated the sort of history of middleclass Western civilization in progress that Condorcet or SaintSimon would have hailed. The progression is not entirely rectilinear, but neither is Turgot's or Condorcet's. In many chapters of the *Reflections on the Philosophy of History* of the 1780s Herder bestowed his blessing on the very development of European arts and sciences that the author of the earlier and more ironic *Still Another Philosophy of History* had derided. The *Reflections* is antidespotic, antimilitary, libertarian, antiaristocratic if not egalitarian, praising of commerce and the mercantile ideal of the independent Riga businessmen among whom Herder found his first post. If the papers on the French Revoluiton, which he never published, are attached to this bourgeois history, the differences between Herder's and Condorcet's history of Europe are much reduced.

Herder's *Völker* are not always as totally compartmentalized as Vico's "nations"; he admits of some diffusion, as Hegel did. Sometimes the chain of culture is cumulative, though only to a small degree since the inner experience of growth and maturity is paramount. The splendor of Europe lies in its activity and inventiveness, its sciences and common striving. When Herder seeks to account for Europe's cultural primacy, he concentrates upon *Kunstfleiss*—Europe is workmanlike and diligent. True, the geography was congenial; the *Klima,* or physical environment, was challenging without being overwhelming; Europe was poor and was stimulated by its needs. But above all it was industriousness that characterized its genius. If Europe had been as rich as India it would not have been goaded by necessity; if it had not been traversed by great rivers it would have been another Tartary; if it had been as isolated as America its real genius would not have come to fruition. But the confluence was perfect. And it was blessed with a rich cultural heritage from Greece and Rome. These were optimum conditions for the flowering of its unique magnificence. A century and a half later Arnold Toynbee would advance a similar theory to explain the genesis of successful civilizations. For all Herder's doctrine of the equality of peoples and nations, in the end he cannot restrain a measure of enthusiasm for Europe. He does not quite trumpet its superiority over all previous embodiments of Humanity, but at moments he surely implies it. Europe is the jewel of mankind.

II

Book 7 of the *Reflections,* published in Leipzig and Riga in 1785, contains the heart of Herder's philosophy of history. Posterior to Kant's essay on universal history (1784), it propounds many related ideas and uses familiar phrases even when the polemical bite is sharp. Herder, at once eclectic and an original genius, never resolved the tension of his relations with his former professor at Königsberg. In this strained association, in which were intermingled experiences of early adoration that reached the dimensions of love for a father-surrogate and later rejection that assumed the feeble intellectual form of Herder's travesty of Kant's *Critique of Pure Reason,* the rational and emotive elements became so intertwined that problems of influence are insoluble. In later years Herder, passionately seeking to establish his own identity, had a compelling need to criticize, attack, differentiate himself; yet he often repeated the same conceptions in his own dithyrambic style.

Herder weaves a tapestry around the ideas of unity and multiplicity in mankind. His opening passage expresses starry-eyed wonderment at the sheer variety of human forms, the millions upon millions of biological differences between the structure of one human being and another, and the infinitely greater number of distinctive psychic phenomena that must pass through these physiological vessels. Between one man and another there may be some external resemblance, but in his inner being each is a separate world. Herder sensed the immediacy and variety of experience. The parts are so different, every individual is subject to so many unique influences from the external world, that the harmony of a human being astounds him. Man like every other component of the natural order is subject to eternal change. Instead of quoting the Heraclitean dictum, Herder prefers to communicate perpetual modification by resorting to the physiologists, who had estimated scientifically that the body of an eighty-year-old man had been renewed more than twenty-four times in the course of his life. If this is true about a single individual, what a continuous process of change the historical world of mankind must be.

But while Herder affirmed the rule of eternal change in man and nature, he never moved in the direction of biological evolutionary theory. Despite all variations, man was a unique and fixed species, a unity in the world distinct from other created forms. In defiance of the evolutionary hypotheses on the philosophical level that were already current in his day, Herder the Pietist dogmatically asserted that man did not shade off into other species that approximated humankind. Man was a creation with attributes not possessed even in embryonic or distorted form by any other animal. Giants were a fiction; the orangutan had no speech; tailed men were a superstition. Alongside these animals and monstrosities men of all races were seen as members of a brotherhood, a single species. Each species had its nature, however diverse its constituents, and was not capable of mixing its blood with any other.

Though moved by the sense of extraordinary diversity among individuals, Herder refused to countenance any race theories that would divide humanity into four or five types with different origins and natures. Kant had been partial to the theory that a set number of races constituted distinct and different human species in the original creation, and Herder's shafts were aimed directly at him. In Herder's thought the key unit of mankind remains the *Volk,* the people, not the race; it is a historical, not a biological, concept. Each *Volk* had its language and national structure, but there were no set boundaries among the various peoples based on different primeval origins. One race gradually passes into another and the totality is a humanity unrelated to other species. "O man, honour thyself: neither the pongo nor the gibbon is thy brother: the american and the negro are: these therefore thou shouldst not oppress, or murder, or steal; for they are men, like thee: with the ape thou canst not enter into fraternity."[8] The various forms of mankind are not parts of a systematic natural history, but constitute a physicogeographical history of man.[9]

The transformations and variations of man are primarily the consequences of geographic location or *Klima,* the word Herder applied to a whole complex of environmental conditions (it is by no means restricted to "climate" in his usage). What happened in history was that a single species, man, acclimatized itself to a wide variety of conditions, which generated a multiplicity of human forms. The *Volk* is continually subject to change with the passage of time. No writer in Western culture (a few pre-Socratic phrases, potent though they may be, should not be overplayed) has struggled more valiantly than Herder to describe the flux of experience. In its native habitat, which means in the geographic area where a nation has lived for thousands upon thousands of years, there is an ideal symbiotic relationship between a *Volk* and its *Klima.* The *Volk* genius really cannot express itself in another habitat. The mass of the *Volk* knows the *Klima* and can live within its confines happily. Driven elsewhere, a *Volk* will in time be transformed by a new environment. Similarly, the *Volk* that remains in its native habitat can be slowly altered in its innermost being if the area in which it lives is changed through either nature or art. The manner of this transformation and its tempo are central problems of the history of culture. The essential *Volk* nature, though subject to change with the passing of generations, at any moment is clearly stamped upon each individual member and is recognizable wherever he may wander.

At the opening of Chapter 3 in Book 7 of the *Reflections* Herder posed one of the basic questions that he constantly tosses at his reader, almost casually. "What is *Klima* and what effect does it have on the formation of body and soul?" In striving to distinguish his theories from Montesquieu's climatological explanation of the spirit of the laws among various nations, Herder, like many others reading Montesquieu simplistically, first reduced his rich thought to its least important formula and then charged that his emphasis upon "heat and cold" was restrictive. Men still knew too little about the consequences of the presence in their midst of mountains, seas, deserts, winds to be able to determine precisely how they affected them, Herder argued, but he did not foreclose the possibility that such discoveries would yet be made. Herder remains the philosopher of autonomous individuality, but no eighteenth-century thinker could completely surrender the illusion that mankind would someday find an underlying pattern beneath the diversity. Despite the low esteem in which systems were held, Herder did not exclude the existence of some ultimate Leibnizian harmony to which men as yet had no access. But for all his own stress upon *Klima* (in the complexity of its meaning), Herder did not consider it the creative drive of his historical unit, the *Volk*. *Klima* altered innate tendencies, but did not determine, did not compel. Its influence was long-term, it worked through the ages, but at a given moment in history its strength could not be assayed. Perhaps eventually its general effects would become identifiable and someone would write a *Spirit of the Klima,* but since the data were not yet available Herder sought the dynamic drive within the *Volk* elsewhere and found it in the *genetische Kraft,* its genetic power. This is the mother of all history; upon it climate may work benignly or hostilely. Yet after the rhetorical sonorities have been let loose, the meaning of genetic power remains something of a sacred mystery.

Herder tries repeatedly to communicate his feeling for the organic existence of man and the *Volk*. He describes in dramatic terms the birth and the nature of a living pulsating organism, confessing that he does not quite know how to define the power that gives life to a creature. He has only a set of adjectives to characterize it: "This capacity is innate, organic, genetic. It is the foundation of my natural powers, the inner genius of my being." [10] Organic power is not reason—of this he is certain; reason is always an alien faculty in an organic body. Herder is not in the *cogito ergo sum* school; he is far nearer to the Romantics and twentieth-century existentialists. I live, therefore I am, he virtually says. For all his later praise of reason as a human attribute, it is the organic force of nature that occupies the center of his philosophy.

The early part of the *Reflections* reaches a climax in an insightful discussion of the tension between *Genesis* and *Klima* that can be generated in the course of history. Both are forces. *Genesis* is the internal creative, organic power that bestows being upon a person or by analogy a *Volk* and makes it possible to distinguish character. *Genesis* imprints character on nature; it is itself not character, but the force that creates it. Herder would accept the science of physiognomy when men had discovered its alphabet and learned to read its truths. This character, this fashioned nature, is not subject to fundamental alteration: The rose cannot become a lily. Since *Klima,* however, can operate on the given character structure of a person or a people and modify it with time, there may be conflict between *Genesis* and *Klima*. *Genesis* is tough, a hard core, refractory to change; it is the creative essence of a man or a people. The *Klima* or environment is an agglomerate of many elements and penetrates from all sides, gradually, sometimes imperceptibly, until it reaches the resistant center of a being and with the aid of habit ultimately succeeds in affecting the core. The national genius is the historical form that results from the operation of the genetic power in men living in a particular *Klima*.

The profound interrelationship between an environment and a *Volk* helped Herder to understand men's ardent attachment to their native soil. Since their biological and psychic structure had been molded by the land, if they were cut off from it they were robbed of a sustaining element. From contemporary travel literature Herder drew heart-rending descriptions of the sufferings of Negroes torn from their native Africa, of Greenlanders brought to Denmark and dying of nostalgia for their homeland. Herder breaks off his theoretical exposition to deliver apostrophes in the spirit of Abbé Raynal against the barbarism of the slave trade. "And what right have you, monsters! even to approach the country of these unfortunates, much less to tear them from it by stealth, fraud and cruelty?"[11] A horrible crime in itself, the slave trade violates the basic unit of historical existence, the nation attached to its

soil. The philosophy of history has a religious and a moral lesson
to teach: To allow the *Volk-Klima* relationship to develop without
interference is the natural manner for historical agents to work.
The organic unfolding of a *Volk* genius then takes place in accordance with an inner rhythm of development. But when outsiders
intervene, when they intrude upon the union of a people and its
agelong inhabited land, they are moving counter to the divine law,
which intends that all organic forces attain full fruition in time.
The alien conquerors are rebels against nature and the divine will
as revealed in the historic process. They are committing sacrilege
against God and history.

The intensity of the *Volk-Klima* feeling is demonstrated by the
sporadic uprisings, the violence of reaction, among primitive peoples against invaders. Foreigners decry the treachery of natives
who pounce upon them after they have made treaties of friendship. What actually occurs is a sudden outburst of *Nationalgefühl*
(national feeling).[12] The cruelties perpetrated by savages against
the Europeans are to be explained not in terms of a different human nature, but as a natural response to the violation of the
Volk's habitat.

If studies of the displacement of peoples, such as barbarian
wanderings and colonial migrations, were undertaken, it might be
possible to formulate laws of the mixture of *Genesis* and *Klima*.
A physicogeographic history of the descent and transformation
of the human race could thus be compiled. Herder still clung desperately to a monogenetic theory of history that conveniently harmonized with sacred history. The world historical problem had
two aspects: an investigation of different environments and the
effects they tended to generate, and an identification of the essential genius of various peoples, a penetration to the inner being of
nations, a stripping of environmentally induced alterations until
the original genius was revealed. Proper studies had not yet been
initiated on a universal scale; but from his own consideration of
recent history Herder in anticipation of the full development of
this science had arrived at a number of general propositions about
the relationship of *Genesis* and *Klima*, propositions applicable in

all times and places. Diversity does not negate fundamental law. And Herder's laws are descriptions that invariably secrete moral precepts.

Rapid transfers of nations from one *Klima* to another of a contrary character have seldom had salutary consequences. This reflection would make the histories of most military conquests, commercial adventures, and missionary activities ludicrous if not tragic. Even the conquerors, the commercial potentates, and the missionaries, full of European arrogance when they first arrived among newly discovered peoples, ended by being swallowed up by the illnesses of the climate; unable to adjust their natures quickly to the strange environment, they languished and died. This was the evidence of the travel literature on the conquest and occupation of the two Indies. It was true also, though to a lesser degree, for North American colonists. The arts of war, for all their violent power, would not be able to convert overnight the new "climates" into areas of European civilization. In the confrontation of environment and *Genesis,* authentic changes required time; ruthless impositions were seldom successful. They led to defeat and death.

The *Genesis* is a whole; it has a structure, a persona: "The entire living creation resides in its integration and this can be tampered with only at great risk."[13] An environment, too, is a structural whole; it cannot be assailed in one of its parts with precipitous violence and no consideration for its organic nature without upsetting the totality. Herder's reading of North American travel literature led him to the conclusion that when the first colonists attacked the forests they rashly altered the natural balance of the climate and made living in the area insalubrious. Burke was to preach a similar lesson with respect to the nature of the nation-state and its reform. "Even in the best work that man can accomplish," wrote Herder, "the settlement of a new land, nature does not like transitions that are too fast, too abrupt."[14]

Even the best should not mature too soon. This is the conclusion of the fourth volume of the *Reflections*. Herder conceived of an optimum pace for the development of *Volk* potentialities—natural, biological time. Condorcet had a vision of improvement at an accelerating rate of speed like a mechanical instrument subject to an ever greater impetus. Herder had an infinite variety of ideal growth times, each appropriate to a different *Volk*. Not all plants and all creatures have the same life cycle and the same rate of growth. What is perfect for one is deadly for another. The environment helps determine what is the fitting rate of growth and so does the original genius. There is no all-embracing universal formula for development except the natural one, which is idiosyncratic. What is natural is what occurs in a given environment when alien elements have not intruded either to stimulate growth artificially or to crush it. Late-twentieth-century theoreticians of the developed and underdeveloped countries of the world are not likely to submit themselves to Herder's ornate rhetoric. But if his ideas made even minor dents in the mechanical analyses of men of power, much human suffering might be alleviated.

Herder used longevity as proof that nature was content with a particular coexistence of human genius and *Klima*. Those who lived as their fathers did lived long; the colonists died young. The American savages who adopted European ways also were cut off early—their *Genesis* and the environment artificially created by the invaders were not compatible. To ask for the statistical evidence for such reflections is to stand condemned as a twentieth-century philistine.

In his hatred of war Herder took a more absolute position than Kant. (For Herder it had served no creative purpose in the past, while Kant found in early war an expression of the cunning of nature ultimately leading to the triumph of reason.) The conquerors were enfeebled by the climate they encountered, corrupted by it, and it required only a weak effort on the part of the subdued people to revolt against them. To the extent that the conquered were forced to adapt themselves to the way of life of the conquerors, they transgressed against their own genius and often became degenerate. War was a deflection of the natural historical or divine design in accordance with which each national spirit should be allowed to dwell peacefully in the habitat where it had grown for centuries, where the genius of the people and its environment had become intertwined with each other in a passionate, life-producing embrace. The genius and the environment were two sexual partners in creation when they were harmonious with each other. But when men of another "genius" migrated, they could do so successfully only if they adapted themselves to the character of the new climate slowly and laboriously. With the passage of time their genius and the influences of the new land might interpenetrate. An organic relationship might be established between the foreign plant and the soil, and genius could again blossom. But if there were any attempt to force unduly the organic processes of nature, disaster would follow and the plant yield only poisoned fruit.

This was a historical conception with a new philosophical assumption about nature and nurture. It did not break with the prevalent eighteenth-century dogma of the unity of mankind or with many aspects of Locke-Condillac sensationalism. But the workings of environment were conceived differently. The environment acted not upon a *tabula rasa* of the soul but upon living creatures who belonged to a *Volk* and already had a genius. Not all environments would immediately exert a benign influence upon this genius and some might even destroy it. Originally mankind was one and perhaps in the end of the days it might again become a unity, but now mankind was many. There was a plurality of peoples and each of the nations had a configuration of its own. If attempts were made to wipe out a primitive way of life and impose European rationalism overnight, the end was likely to be complete annihilation. The processes of culture were organic, not mechanical. The underlying metaphor had been replaced.

To the French sensationalists the process of historical change was not dependent on the passage of long periods of time. Each creature was born anew as a clean slate, and revolutions in human nature were quite possible if new forces exercised themselves upon the person early enough or if methods could be devised to rid societies of the encrustations of stagnant customs and prejudice. Through arts and sciences Europeans could remake the world; an enlightened despot, if he wielded enough power, might alter the beliefs and way of life of his people in accordance with the simple rules of philosophy, irrespective of whether they were Frenchmen, Russians, or Magyars. Time and the processes of time had produced the lies of tradition, but these could be removed quickly by the grand sweep of reason. The French Revolutionaries operated on this assumption, and so did nineteenth-century British imperialists. At the cost of great suffering both those who rule empires and those who have emancipated themselves from Western hegemony may have begun, but only begun, in the late twentieth century to reject Enlightenment shibboleths and to recognize the cogency of Herder's precepts.

III

For all the multiplicity of forms in the human species, men everywhere have the same senses. But important differences exist among peoples in the quality of their sense perceptions, and these are explicable in terms of the influence of *Klima* working through time. From Albrecht von Haller's writings on physiology and from contemporary travel literature, Herder garnered a long list of illustrations to demonstrate the wide variations in the functioning of the senses among different nations: the tolerance of extreme heat and cold among American Indians, the acuity of the olfactory organs of the East Indians. The purpose of these descriptions was to show that there was no intrinsic superiority in the European combination of sense perceptions over those of nations on other continents; they were merely different. The same held true for the habits of peoples. Many Asiatic nations far surpassed Europeans in the virtues of cleanliness and moderation. In the spirit of Rousseau, Herder contrasted unfavorably the continual excitation to which the sensibilities of Europeans were subjected, their consumption of alcohol, for example, with the calm of nations that prohibited the use of stimulants. In Herder's scale of sensibility the highest rank was accorded peoples who were the most delicate and moderate in consumption. By this criterion Europeans did not figure near the top in the order of nations. They gorged and stupefied themselves, dulling their senses rather than sharpening them.

Herder's primitives are amplifications of Rousseau's natural man before the tragic fall in the "second stage" analyzed in the *Discourse on the Origin of Inequality*. Most of them are endowed with finely developed sense organs and live a blissful existence in the present, unbefuddled by reason. There is one art they all possess, music, which expresses their innermost nature more profoundly than any art they later acquire. Music is even more characteristic of a nation than speech, surely more than other external manifestations of a civilization.[15] Herder was one of the first Romantic philosophers to raise music to the highest level of creativity and to make of it the essential clue to the genius of a nation. By appreciating its music one penetrated to the most profound depths of its soul. In music, far more than in rational philosophy and institutions, lay buried the secret genius of nations. Vico had discovered it in poetry, in law, in customs, in all the multifarious expressions of man. Herder had an implied hierarchy of creativity: Music and its outgrowth poetry were the truest revelations of the national ethos.

Herder had a historical conception of plenitude. To use his favorite musical analogy, the nations of the earth were like combinations of tones played upon the harp. National entities were all the harmonies that had been and could have been produced. Nations existed because nature in its fullness had to give birth in time to all possible harmonies. If a conceivable chord was not ultimately sounded this would be a flaw in the perfection of nature and a deficiency in nature's God. History was the record of the necessary creation of nations with distinctive patterns, characters, geniuses, of all the possible harmonies of which nature was capable.

Each of the national harmonies was by its very constitution incapable of truly comprehending the others. Greenlanders could understand the beliefs of European nations only by analogy to their own. National fantasies, the mythologies of the nations, were landscapes of their souls, distinctive, almost impossible to communicate one to another. Mythology to Herder was no longer mere nonsense, babbling superstition, "prejudice" in the eighteenth-century meaning. A myth was the first philosophic effort of the human soul to grasp reality, to explain, to perceive the environment in which a nation dwelled. It was the spontaneous creation of the early interaction of a national genius with its *Klima*. Hence the particular character of each nation's mythology, a primitive people's unique rendering of its own reality. The rituals of medicine men, magicians, and shamans were not the fabrications of "deceivers." They were rather mirrors of the external world as perceived by a folk at an early stage in its development, and through the transmission of traditions and education the tribal leaders were able to perpetuate this way of experiencing the world. Vico had arrived at the same idea—his conception of poetic wisdom—half a century earlier, but there is no evidence that Herder knew of Vico in 1785, though he wrote of him with sympathetic understanding at a later period.

Herder saw in fantasy, in the imagination, the still unexplored power of the soul of nations. He did not disdain primitives as men living in the outer darkness. As a philosophical moralist, he sought to humble the pride of Europeans, their feeling of superiority over the primitive peoples whom they had conquered. The Europeans may have demonstrated a greater development of rationalist capacities, but other nations were superior in poetry and art. Herder's history of man is not the progress of rational scientific knowledge, preferably in mathematical form, as with Condorcet. Nor is it a history of the ethicization of man and the repression of the instinctual, as wtih Kant. History is an expression of the multiple harmonies of nations, and among most of them the imaginative faculties and fantasies were far more potent than the rational element, a reversal of the Greek values as they had been amalgamated with theological Christianity.

The Enlightenment of the West represented clarity through analysis, mathematics, the abstract being the most perfect creation. Herder and his friend Hamann stood for the organic, the poetic, the passionate, the complex, even the murky, if the images touched the emotions. Abstraction was an empty shell. Where was the ultimate truth to be discovered? In mathematical thinking or in the most ancient records of the race, the first impress of divine truth?

The pastor Herder read the Bible as a revelation, but also as the oldest historical document of the Jewish people. Spinoza had preceded him in the seventeenth century with the *Tractatus Theologico-Politicus,* the fountainhead of modern heresy. The crucial difference between them lay in the nature of the history that they discovered in the Bible. Spinoza made of the Old Testament a social and political document that embodied the rational wisdom of the great legislator of the Hebrews. For Herder, the Bible was a projection of the soul of the inspired ancient Hebrews, the first people to express in poetic language the relations of man and God, of man and nature, a prototype for the mythologies of all the peoples of the earth. The concreteness of biblical imagery, its reflection of the religious spirit in a specific "oriental" environment, was not a limitation of the sublime. Men had to couch their thoughts and feelings in geographic and physical terms. When a theologically minded Newtonian read the word *earth* in the Bible, he thought of the abstract sphere of the physicist. By contrast, in Herder's commentary "earth" meant the real earth of which man's primitive hut was molded and the earth of the worms to which he returned. It had color and texture. The Bible, like all primitive creations, was continually evoking the actual experience of man. The darkness of Genesis was a thick reality, not a metaphysical emptiness. "Whoever on the desolate open seas, surrounded by night and the fear of death, has hoped for the dawn, he has felt this tangible blackness." [16]

IV

The attitude of an eighteenth-century man toward the nature and history of language is a clue to his religious position and his view of worldly progression. Vico, Hamann, and Turgot would have stood together in the conviction that language contained within it the true history of mankind's stadial development from primitive times to the Enlightenment. But the accord among them ends there. Vico looked upon the Enlightenment movement toward abstract rational speech as an inevitable accompaniment of the humanization process, though he was at once appreciative of the sensate language of early barbarism and fearful of the refinements of the last stages before the coming of the hypersophisticated barbarians of the intellect. Turgot longed for the age when the movement from emotive language to symbolic abstraction would reach its ultimate goal in the creation of a universal mode of scientific notation, from which the obscurities of feeling would be banished forever. In revulsion against this idealization of the mathematical, Hamann and Herder viewed every attempt to introduce general terms as a sign of degeneration, decadence, dehumanization. Progress for them meant restoration of the primitive sensibility and forms of expression before the desiccation of metaphysical abstractions had set in.

Once Herder had recovered from his youthful flirtation with rationalist philosophy under the tutelage of Kant in Königsberg, his theory of religious origins relied upon a mixture of theology and history. Religion was no longer a naturalistic phenomenon, but a revelation, a divine intervention in an even more intimate sense than Vico's birth of the gods. The revelation, however, was clothed in a variety of historic forms among different nations, so that it was never divested of naturalistic elements. God revealed Himself anew each time a national entity was born. In the Judeo-Christian world His revelation was most complete. It was emotionally all-embracing because the tongue of the Hebrews chosen by Him was a perfect vehicle for the communication of religious truth and the genius of the place an ideal background for the enactment of the drama. This revelation was not a unique occurrence, however; with variations the performance was repeated again and again in the earliest moments of each *Volk* existence.

Among the Jews, the Bible was the Word of God made flesh; among the Gentiles, revelation assumed different forms. Egyptian hieroglyphs and Greek religious mysteries were symbolic divine manifestations of the same order, local variations depending upon the physical landscape that had originally shaped the soul of the people. "That the Egyptian hieroglyphs deal with knowledge of the gods and of nature, only a Warburtonian head can deny."[17]

Through sinfulness and the vice of sensuality the divine revelation to the heathens was rendered impure, but in its origins a pagan mystery was a sublime truth clothed in national costume. When Hamann and Herder defended the worth of mystery religions, they were at the same time aiming polemical darts at those of their German contemporaries who interpreted the pagan rituals as prefigurations of Christianity or a stage in the progressive ethicization of man. The mysteries were not academies of natural religion à la Johann August von Starck, the author of a *De Tralatitiis ex gentilismo in religionem christianam* (*On Transmissions from Paganism to the Christian Religion*), whose appointment to the Faculty of Theology in Königsberg had outraged Hamann, nor schools of rational philosophy, nor ancient Freemasonic lodges, nor a stage in Lessing's *Die Erziehung des Menschengeschlechts* (1780). The mystery religion of an ancient people had embodied the whole of divinity, even though the form was corrupt; religious truth was not instilled in driblets and was no more subject to rational improvement than was language. Religion in any people was a total creation, not a partial one; it might be polluted, but it was not subject to Lockian progression, to development through experience.

In the late 1760s and the 1770s Herder was already attacking the *philosophes* for their abstract conceptions of the primitive that were presumed to apply equally to all lands throughout the world, while he had begun to see primitive minds expressed in myths as reflections of particular geographic situations. French theorists of primitive religion were merely projecting their rationalist, hypersophisticated selves into the primitive world, instead of comprehending the emotional, sensuous character of early peoples. A primitive *Volk* was bound to its limited geographic area, and its poetic imagery reflected not universal ideas but a particular landscape. Nicolas Boulanger's monistic theory of the origins of all myths in the memory of a universal deluge was an easy object for Herder's mockery in the *Fragmente zu einer Archäologie des Morgenlandes* (*Fragments for an Archaeology of the East*), 1769—
"The deluge is everywhere that there is water, wherever water is

poured, wherever one washes with water."[18] For Herder, the waters of the Egyptian religious myth were not recollections of a universal deluge but evocations of the flooding of a specific river, the Nile. Each primitive poetry had a quality not repeated elsewhere. Herder declaimed with the conviction of a man who knew the peasants of the Slavic world, on whose border lands he had studied and worked. The gods were symbols of nature—not rationalist allegories. They expressed the world of primitive men whose senses were more acute than their reason, who were close to the earth and its creatures, who felt themselves an integral part of organic nature and kindred to all living things. The early religions, like primitive poetry, embodied experience of the immediate physical environment into which men were born. Herder's primitive religion was not a product of fear alone or of rational perception. It was a translation of the whole of early man's world in a given *Klima*.

Since Charles de Brosses, author of *Du culte des dieux fétiches* (*On the Worship of Fetish Gods*), had raised the problem of Egyptian brute-worship, Herder felt obliged to fit its practices into his system. He too was against allegorical interpretations of zoolatry, but while de Brosses could not contemplate this cult without revulsion even when he explained it, Herder eulogized it as the adoration of life force. God created man among animals, the primitive Egyptians lived in close proximity to their beasts, they knew their spirit and their feelings. "We? What is an animal to us? In our palaces, in our discussion clubs, in our stone edifices withdrawn from everything in nature, what is an animal to us? Who looks upon it except for play or pleasure or for system-making? Who can sense invisible divinity in the beast and learn brotherhood from him? But look here, my dear book-and-tickle-philosopher, just ask the simple countryman, the shepherd, the hunter, inquire of the times of Aesop, of Homer, of the dawn of the primitive world what an animal was to man! . . . Your 'développement des arts et des sciences' is far more philosophical and finer—Good! Go see what the man who lives among animals still learns and observes from them."[19] The animal worship of the Egyptians was neither Athanasius Kircher's theology in disguise, nor hieroglyphic writing divinized, nor African fetishism. The early Egyptians lived in a world of nature where the separation of man from animal and plant life was not as marked as among civilized city-dwellers. Primitive men, like shepherds and countryfolk in all ages, could communicate with animals, learn from their ways, understand their language. They perceived the divine in every living creature and in every organic growth. The Egyptian worship of the phallus was a natural adoration of divine creative power and obviously would not be comprehended by the coy virgins of France.

Any philosophic document of the past that lent itself even remotely to this outlook was drawn into Herder's net (whatever the intentions of the author may have been). Spinoza's pantheism, for example, his apparent repudiation of the matter-spirit dichotomy, and the emotional quality of his conception of God attracted Herder to him. From Leibniz Herder derived the feeling for continuous process, the sense of individuation, and the glorification of the particular in a world harmony that are so vital for modern historical consciousness.

VI

Herder enlarged the historical vision in a spectacular manner. Reading French philosophical histories from Turgot through Comte, one is impressed with their fundamental Europocentrism and the finiteness, even narrowness, of their appreciation of "otherness." Herder cherished the individuality of each *Volk* or agglomeration of people, wherever and whenever it had appeared, and recognized its equivalent (or almost equivalent) status in the history of mankind. Any body of men that formed a fresh cultural configuration was a noble manifestation of God's creativity, of power, of energy, of nature—the particular rhetorical choice varies from passage to passage.

In bestowing significance upon the history of all peoples, Herder rather consistently refused to indulge in comparisons among them. Each *Volk* carried the principle of its individuality within itself; it was a self-contained Leibnizian monad. The Christian pietist conception of souls equal in the eyes of God was extended to peoples throughout world history.

In broad acceptance of the infinite variety of human cultures, Herder broke out of traditional religious and political molds that had confined Christian Europeans for centuries. He has no antecedents of comparable vigor and few descendants. In fact his vision was so large that it failed to sustain itself in German thought. Kant bluntly rejected it from the outset, and Hegel, too, outrightly denied history to the primitive, waiting for the emergence of an organized state before he would deign to consider a cultural form as an admissible embodiment of Spirit. In this respect Marx did not follow Hegel, and there are idealizations of patriarchal society in his writings to which Hegel would never have subscribed, though Marx paused at this early stage only as a way station to a utopian condition of man, not as worthy in itself.

The history of the world for Herder is the history of the *Völker*— their emergence as a consequence of the interpenetration of their physical environment and their being, and their creation of a mythic cosmology, a music, a poetry, and above all, a language. The union of their original nature, their genius, and the environment reaches a climax in a form-giving moment—it is not quite clear whether this is the awareness of religious or of linguistic identity. But there is no stasis. The process of change is continuous as long as the people is alive. It may become subject to disruption during the course of its wanderings to a new environment; it may suffer the evils of invasion; and inevitably it will die. Some cultures outlive themselves, dragging themselves about monotonously until they become stinking corpses. (Hegel would adapt this concept without acknowledgment.) But except for the cultures that outlast their creative capacity, Herder makes all moments of time in all cultures worthy of respect. His was a Christianization of the historic process as well as democratization to a degree that had never been achieved before. As nineteenth- and twentieth-century intellectuals in Central Europe read Herder, they found in his work a justification for the independence of the embryonic nations to which they belonged, and he became the chosen philosopher of the Slavophiles and the new cultural nationalism that destroyed the Hapsburg Empire.

There is an ideal, natural way to self-fulfillment for each *Volk* analogous to an individual's development from birth to the grave. Unfortunately, peoples have foresaken their natural home, have destroyed and been destroyed, have contaminated other cultures and been contaminated. The subjection of cultures to the vicissitudes of such experience are the tragic, unnatural episodes of world history. The monad of *Volk* individuality can be and has been lost. That which is mixed is rarely good, that which imitates is a defilement, and that which is forced lacks authenticity. Somehow a culture can never survive imperial extension.

Among the classical philosophers of history Herder was perhaps the most richly intuitive. Eschewing a traditional Western European and Greco-Roman fixation, which has persisted well into our century among historians, he pushed the geographic dimensions of the historical in all directions. The historical included the primitive as well as the civilized, and the aboriginal was not a mere prelude to the more advanced. Every moment of historical experience was precious. Moreover, Herder's history was not confined to rational intent and to action directed primarily by the state. He invented the concept of the national soul, defined and described in feeling tones, not in terms of power relations. The cultural emanations of peoples rather than their political acts were the stuff of history. Masterpieces of religion, music, poetry, and art became history's major events and central significance. Science and technology, too, played a role, but of lesser importance. Emotion took its place alongside reason—perhaps it even assumed a position of primacy as a creative force. In Herder, cultural history is no longer on sufferance, boxed and isolated in a few sections at the end of a chronicle of royal exploits, after the manner of Voltaire. Herder turned conventional history writing upside down, relegating the political and military to the lower end of the table, to be devalued and demeaned as lesser manifestations of the human spirit.

There was a period in the 1930s when, under the influence of Marx's thought, many historians tended to underplay the role of the *Volk* or the nation as the vehicle best suited to an understanding of history. The economic system, or system of production-relations, under which were subsumed so many peoples, seemed a more compelling unit of existence. The aggressive nation-state was looked upon as a latecomer in the modern historical process, destined to be swallowed up in the dramatic confrontation of world capitalism and revolutionary world communism. This crude polarization blinded men to the tenacious vitality of national cultures, irrespective of whether the prevailing socioeconomic system could be labeled capitalist, communist, socialist, or some combination of the three. Politically, the ruling potentates of the most powerful capitalist and communist states have repeatedly erred in underestimating the vigor of cultural collectives within their spheres of influence. Despite lipservice to national rights, it has been assumed that they were not autonomous sources of great psychic potency and that these spiritual forces could be manipulated with ease. One does not have to neglect the ideological hegemony of the socioeconomic system to acknowledge that the bonds of the nation are far mightier than internationalists imagined in the period between the two World Wars. Attempts to impose alien socioeconomic forms that run counter to deep-rooted religious and national traditions have met resistance astounding to those who imagined that in human collectives the slate of historical experience could be wiped clean by the fiat of political or military power.

Today Herder, the dithyrambic, Pietist preacher who appreciated the hard core of primitive *Volk*-spirit, has to be studied with a new attentiveness. Even the most ruthless tyrants have had to bow before the strength of national and *Volk* community. It may be that after many ages the end of isolation will weaken the national spirit; but in the latter part of the twentieth century the traditional forces seem to have re-emerged in forms that are often archaic, sometimes comical, even vicious, but never negligible. Scientific reason may vaunt its universal triumphs, but man the willing, feeling creature is still dependent on small units of social and psychic existence.

7 THE TRIADIC METAPHOR

I N an episode of his *True Story* Lucian of Samosata indiscrimi-
nately tossed the great philosophical and military heroes of
antiquity onto the Island of the Blessed and recounted with malicious delight the ensuing entanglements among them. Plato was
the exception. Lucian took care to isolate him in a republic he had
constructed for himself in accordance with a constitution and
laws of his own devising. In imitation of Lucian I have gathered
together a select group of thinkers of the second half of the eighteenth century who believed in the coming of a heaven on earth,
leaving Jean-Jacques Rousseau alone on a platform floating above
them. Though he would have excluded them from his *monde idéal,*
with one or two chronological exceptions they all lived in the
shadow of his creation.

Apart from Rousseau, my community will not be dominated by
the *patres majores* of the French and English Enlightenment,
whose attitude toward an ideal state of the soul, a eupsychia, or
an optimum society for that matter, was at best ambivalent, and
often downright negative.[1] The incorrigible Diderot never really
believed in his Lampedusa, any more than Voltaire did in his
El Dorado; nor did Montesquieu have faith in his Troglodytes.
There is not even an article on utopia in the *Encyclopédie,* and
Grimm and Meister regularly demeaned the whole genre with the
disdainful epithet *espèce d'utopie.*

My assemblage is limited to men committed to the possibility of
an ideal state of the soul in this world, men who were either indifferent to or skeptical about the existence of the soul in the next

one, despite the fact that many of them had worn clerical habit at some time in their lives. On my island each one bears the symbol of his inspiration or his achievement. Morelly, anonymous as ever, a man without a Christian name, carries aloft his *Code de la nature* (1755). They used to believe he was Diderot and now they conjecture that he may have been Dom Deschamps, though I doubt it. Whoever he is, here he is treated as a person in his own right. Dom Deschamps holds in one hand a replica of the Benedictine monastery outside of Saumur where he was a *gros bonnet* for many years and in the other a copy of *Le Vrai système*.[2] The Curé Meslier, who died before Rousseau began to thunder, proudly displays a twentieth-century edition of his manuscripts—he has finally acquired a separate identity and has been cleansed of the emendations of the Holbach synagogue.[3] The Abbé Mably makes a dramatic entrance appropriately clad in Spartan dress. These occasional worshipers of the Catholic God are joined by a dissenting clergyman from England, William Godwin, who is lugging the two weighty volumes of *Political Justice* (1793). Restif de la Bretonne, son of a severe Jansenist peasant-farmer, perched atop the five ponderous tomes of his *Idées singulières* (1769–1789) that promise to bring about the happiness of mankind, is busy caressing a little shoe. The Marquis de Sade, the most militant atheist in the assembly, is accompanied by an *historienne,* as were the heroes in *Les Cent vingt journées de Sodome;*[4] she is laden down with a model of the Bastille, where he did his best work, and a charred copy of the manuscript *La Nature dévoilée,* burned by his priggish son. Turgot, once an abbé in the Sorbonne, allows his atheistic disciple Condorcet to do most of the talking; they have the self-satisfied look of prophets fulfilled. In a far corner sit the Germans with studious gravity. Immanuel Kant stares at the signpost of an inn that depicts a cemetery and is inscribed *Eternal Peace.*[5] Lessing bears a Freemasonic triangle and the hundred theses of his *Education of the Human Race* (1780). Schiller looks perplexed as he reads his own *Aesthetic Letters.* Finally, two young men, Saint-Just and Babeuf, the former an adept of Robespierre's Cult of the Supreme Being, the latter an atheist of the Sylvain

Maréchal stripe, are carrying their heads underneath their arms. The rest of the group tends to avoid them as too involved with practical utopistics and not good enough at the theory of the ideal state of the soul.

A first reaction to this assembly might well be "Quelle galère!" And yet the selection was by no means arbitrary.

I

The eupsychias of Enlightenment thinkers were secular modifications of the third phase in a stadial metaphor that has its origins in the division of worldly time in early Judaism and Christianity: the age of the Garden of Eden or the first paradise, this world of suffering or the vale of tears, followed at last by the days of the Messiah or a thousand-year reign of Christ on earth. In both Jewish and Christian apocalyptic literature, the evils of this world are exacerbated on the eve of a terrifying, destructive age of transition between stages two and three. The stadial metaphor was renewed among unorthodox Christian thinkers of the Middle Ages, as in Joachim of Fiore's three states, each of which generated a different psychic character in man, and among millenarian thinkers of the Radical Reformation like Thomas Münzer, who distinguished an original paradise from the present reign of the fleshly and the spiritual union of a new kingdom yet to be. With the intrusion of science into the seventeenth-century Christian utopia, the stages were altered to a paradisaical age of perfect knowledge, a fall into ignorance, and finally a restoration to the prelapsarian condition through the propagation of the knowledge of God in things and a radical "emendation of human affairs." Before the Enlightenment, the three phases could either stand in a dialectical relationship of contrariety to one another, or they could represent some form of linear progression.

While the eupsychias of the second half of the eighteenth century preserve the triadic pattern of the religious metaphor, they infuse it with new meanings. Stripped of religious language, the original paradise becomes either the state of nature or sometimes the state of savagery, the Fall is a drop into a morass called civilization, and the redemption is a translation into a third stage which is the eupsychia. The eupsychia is a state of metaphysical and moral wholeness for mankind. Deschamps calls it the *état de moeurs;* Lessing, the Third Age, the modified eternal gospel of the Joachites; Condorcet, an Elysium created by reason; Rousseau, the *monde idéal.*

Many of the eupsychians of the latter half of the eighteenth century have been assimilated into the history of thought as precursors of socialism or communism. But they have a separate being of their own—only in retrospect does one become a precursor. They may in fact propose radical political, economic, and social changes—the abolition of private property or of monogamous sexual possession—as complements of a new human psychic condition. Since they were not burdened with either great interest in or understanding of the realities of the economic process, these eupsychians focused primarily upon the psychological consequences of the privatization of objects, both persons and things. Their diagnosis of the sickness of the age takes place on the moral, religious, and psychological level, and the demonstration of the cure is on the same plane. With two glaring exceptions, my headless revolutionaries Saint-Just and Babeuf, conversion to faith in the eupsychia occurs through the persuasiveness of the word and the dialectical movement of history.

While the eupsychians are ignorant of the keen eighteenth-century analysts of the economic process working in France and England, their writings are usually made of sterner stuff than the flood of speaking-picture utopias in the Morean manner—the *voyages imaginaires, robinsonades,* and *romans cabalistiques* that inundated the continent. With some effort, a compendium of the standard moral values preached by the *philosophes* could be distilled from this organic mass, this *magna turba,* of utopianizing fiction. At some time in the course of his many harrowing experiences the conventional hero of one of these tales comes upon a good natural society and here a utopia is inserted. Most of the stories may be compared to the Hellenistic utopian novels, of which a few fragments have survived. In their empty activism they suggest the drying-up of an inner life among readers who resorted to this vapid literature. Their eupsychian element is thin and the religious underpinning of their heaven on earth is meager.

My taxonomy of the authentic eupsychian species begins with Jean-Jacques, who defies categorization, moves on to a group of ascetic communal eupsychians, for whom the condition of absolute equality is the key to an ideal psychological existence, stops by a few shady characters who point to the fulfillment of man's sexual nature as the key to his happiness, and comes to rest with alternative visions on the two sides of the Rhine, a utopia of rationalist social science in France and a utopia informed by a moral-aesthetic ideal in Germany.

II

The grand thaumaturge of the eupsychian movement was Jean-Jacques. His diagnostic pronouncements, if not his pretentious remedies, can still intoxicate anyone who takes a few big draughts. Others had preceded Rousseau in describing *le mal moral;* but once he spoke, the minor prophets who succeeded him could never struggle free of his rhetoric. One can hear its reverberations in documents as diverse as the writings of Kant and the youthful correspondence of Babeuf, not to speak of Deschamps, Restif, de Sade, Godwin, and, in the next epoch, Marx.

Rousseau had a genius for transforming his fantasies into brilliant, rationalist structures. He delineates the healthy psychological attributes of man in the state of nature, describes the anguish of the present "difforme contraste," and then proposes to reincorporate the characteristics of the original state into the third state, on a higher level. Without benefit of Giambattista Vico, Rousseau knew that language followed the vicissitudes of morals and was altered with them. Each phase had its own unique speech expressive of its mentality. The eupsychians of the eighteenth century did not quite utter the words of Vico, *tre spezie di nature,* but they were thinking in similar terms. At one time the emotive cry of primitive language was not dissociated from the object it signified; in the miserable intermediary present state, the disjuncture is complete; in the future, language will again be authentically reflective of the feeling evoked by objects. Once action was in measured balance with desire; now it is in complete imbalance; in the future action will proceed only from real desire.

Throughout his life Rousseau kept commenting upon the three phases of mankind's existence, in the Discourses, in *La Nouvelle Héloïse,* in the *Social Contract,* in *Emile,* in the *Rêveries.* The contradictions that he discovered in societal man are surely not absent from his own texts spread over a quarter of a century. In our time, there has grown up a corpus of brilliant commentary on Jean-Jacques's commentaries, each expositor of Rousseau singling out his favorite passages. I am rather partial to the version in *Rousseau juge de Jean-Jacques,* his very last work, though Saint-Preux's description of Paris in *La Nouvelle Héloïse* and the end of the Second Discourse are probably the prophet's most devastating indictments of civilization in its final stages of decay.

Early in *Rousseau juge de Jean-Jacques,* the protagonist of the dialogue calls upon *Le François* to imagine an ideal world resembling the one he lived in, yet essentially different. The physical nature of the earth remains fundamentally unchanged; but the emotions of all its inhabitants are mysteriously heightened, the arrangement of things is more perfect, forms are more elegant, colors brighter, odors more subtle. All objects excite admiration. Without benefit of psychedelic drugs Rousseau conjures up a world of nature so strikingly beautiful that it alters the human beings who dwell in it. Instead of the suspicious, cruel, plotting creatures familiar to us, men are suddenly aglow with love for one another. The source of the metamorphosis is nature itself. Men are inspired to place themselves in harmony with its glories and are fearful only lest the dross of their presence contaminate the beauties of the natural world. Human beings acquire a new, more acute sensibility that affords them immediate, exquisite pleasures hitherto unknown. As among Rousseau's contemporaries, the passions are still the driving forces behind all action in the *monde idéal;* but passions have become simpler, purer, livelier, and more ardent. Even among the benighted creatures of present society, original impulses are good and are directed toward self-preservation and happiness. But in the world of today these spontaneous initial feelings bump up against a thousand obstacles as they seek fulfillment and they are diverted from their straight path. The emotions become so tangled in their circuitous attempts to overcome the impediments in their way that they never reach their goals and men forget what the object of their desire was in the first place.

The soul of modern man, the seat of his will, has grown soft and weak so that it is only feebly responsive to the impulse of nature. As a consequence, when the soul in action hits its first obstacle, the will is sharply deflected from its original purpose—Rousseau uses the image of a billiard ball striking a wall and moving off at an angle. But in the *monde idéal* men have strong, willful souls and are like balls shot out of a cannon: They fly straight and either crash through the object they aim for or are shattered by it. In our miserable world men sidestep objects so often that they may finally end up somewhere relatively safe, but it is somewhere else, far from the place they had set out for.

In the *monde idéal* there will be total conformity among feelings, words, and actions—that is the essential definition of the eupsychia. In our world these three basic forms of human expression are totally and constantly at odds with one another. It is in talk about feeling that the contemporary contradiction is most flagrant. No man of sensibility can remotely comprehend what people in Paris salons, with their *jargon de société,* are chattering about. The characters of *La Nouvelle Héloïse* speak the straightforward language of passion of the *monde idéal,* whatever the consequences. In their utopia of Clarens the five protagonists sometimes even return to the silence of the state of nature, when creatures communicated without words.

III

For contrast with Rousseau's *monde idéal,* let me jump to another holistic eupsychia, the Marquis de Sade's *La Philosophie dans le boudoir* (1795), which at once derives from Rousseau and sounds like a veritable parody of his ideas. The five protagonists the Marquis has brought together in a bedroom cannot stop their babble even in the midst of their sexual bouts, though their raunchy speech is totally integrated with their action. In their own way de Sade's characters realize the Rousseauan harmony of feeling (powerful sexual desire), words (a lascivious speech describing it), and actions (the concert of multifaceted sexual activity), but on a level of physical concreteness.

The solitary Benedictine Dom Deschamps, who in 1761 tried in vain to convert Rousseau to his *vrai système,* was in the classical utopian mold. For him Rousseau was a prodromus. His own system was unique, radical; it went to the roots of things, and would found moral behavior on the indisputable metaphysical principle of wholeness. It was constructive, not merely destructive. The prevalent Encyclopedist philosophy might bring about a revolution in religion, manners, and government, but it could do nothing more with its demi-enlightenment. This kind of revolution was as dangerous as it was useless.

Deschamps was in one sense a hangover from the seventeenth century. He was a great system-builder, with the aspirations of a Bacon or a Comenius, a man who held the key to the enigma of all being. Rousseau had failed to draw the moral and philosophical consequences of his spontaneous insights. Deschamps's version of the civil war that raged in the breast of everyman living in the present wretched state of civilization, the *état des lois,* is often clumsy, even ungrammatical. But his doctrine is an arresting example of Rousseau's eupsychia driven to a conclusion from which Jean-Jacques withdrew in terror. The system has the attraction of being metaphysically complete and absolute. Our laws rein in our natural drives and constantly oppose them; but the drives, seeking to go their own way, rise in revolt. The result is a state of violence. We are in perpetual contradiction with ourselves and with one another. We are always suspicious, masked, pained. We go about fearing our own kind, and we end up doing them harm either to avenge what they *did* to us or to prevent what they *might* do to us. Desire, frustration, pointless aggression against imaginary threats poison our lives. If this moral sickness is displayed by the side of psychic health, who would not prefer the new state of morality to the old? It does not matter whether a man is a prince or a peasant, the degenerate *état des lois* today holds him in its grip. Men are like galley slaves under the rod of master-kings. But, adds Deschamps anticipating the reflections of the aged Diderot and Hegel, in many respects the master-kings must grovel before their own subjects when they seek their favor. Deschamps addressed himself with fervor to the literate *philosophes* who were his fellow sufferers, exhorting them to heed his counsel and to accept a system of perfect unity over the face of the whole earth, with men equal, communal, mutually strengthened, and, as if in afterthought, against all the other species. No one more or less happy than another was the only psychic state in which one could enjoy happiness without fear of another. No envy and no jealousy. With a felicitous admixture of Pascal and Rousseau, Deschamps condemns men's frantic struggle to acquire knowledge of more and more things as an evasion, a vain attempt to get outside of their suffering selves, while inside there is chaos, a mass of battling ideas and interests that never leave them at peace.

That man had always sought tranquillity Deschamps proved from the myths of the golden age, paradise, the age of Astraea, pastoral literature, all of which he interpreted as psychologically authentic documents revelatory of human yearning under the present corrupt state of the laws. The future state of morality would be far simpler. It would be denuded of the flowery paraphernalia of paradisaical fantasies; it would be actual.

For Deschamps the difference between appearance and reality is nowhere more stark than in *our* (and by *our* he means the upperclass intellectuals for whom he is writing) view of the lower classes. We treat them roughly and think we are better off than they are; in fact we suffer psychically far more than they do. And they have far less need of the *état de moeurs,* the ideal state, than we *philosophes* do. Deschamps is the self-appointed apostle to the tortured intellectual: Cast off your psychic woes in the only way possible, by establishing an order without property and moral inequality.

When Deschamps finally got around to it, he unveiled the particularities of his eupsychia, one that would hardly have appeased the needs of the guests at the Baron d'Holbach's sumptuous dinner table, despite Diderot's fleeting enthusiasm for Deschamps's world without *meum* and *tuum*. Deschamps envisaged a society divided into communal groups where all men and women would live together in one hut, work together at simple tasks, eat vegetarian food together, and sleep together in one big bed of straw. No books, no writing, no art—all that would be burned. The example of a father would be sufficient teaching for children. There would be no *hommes cultivés* to live parasitically off the poor. The anti-intellectualism of Rousseau is driven to its ultimate conclusion by Deschamps, even as de Sade in *his* eupsychia drew Rousseau's longing for heightened passionate sensibility to its extreme end.

Deschamps's *état de moeurs* provides a happy physical existence. In a prefiguration, or caricature, of Marx's *Gotha Program Critique,* he expressly condemns the present separation of mental and physical labor which he eliminates by abolishing intellectuals, and he rules out the specialization of physical labor by having workers pass from one simple task to another. Work is indistinguishable from pleasure or amusement. There will be no factitious entertainments, only the fulfillment of the *true needs of man.* Groups freely joined in labor and love cooperate with one another, but unlike Rousseau's *monde idéal,* Deschamps's is a low-keyed eupsychia, without passions, without distinctions between men and women, without outbursts of laughter or crying. Sexual appetites will be appeased with no more ado than eating, drinking, sleeping. One day is as happy as the next. Children belong to society and they learn to perform with their hands all necessary tasks, including elementary surgery. Mothers give freely of their milk to the young and the very old. Language becomes purified, simple, and absolutely stable, since there is no changing intellectual or emotional substance for speech to reflect. (Thus passes the department of linguistics.) The eupsychic state has *douce sérénité, candeur naïve, simplicité aimable,* and at the end a *mort douce.* There will be no mourning because there has been no great emotional investment in any individual.

The metaphysical underpinning to Deschamps's system has intrigued the modern French philosopher Jean Wahl. The attraction that moves human beings toward their principle, which is the whole and is an entity that is different from the sum of its parts, is of the same order as the movement of inanimate things to their center. The contrary force is the spirit of independence—individuation. Private possession of land and women introduced the moral evil disrupting the natural tendency toward union and wholeness. Universal union is man's true principle. In a dialectical movement man has been destined to pass stadially from the condition of savage nature, through the social state of *laws,* to the true system of the *état de moeurs,* or the truth.

Deschamps tried hard to peddle his *vrai système* among the *philosophes.* Rousseau flirted with him in 1761 and 1762 but refused to read the text beyond the preface, since Deschamps could not guarantee that it would make him happier. Diderot saw Deschamps three or four times in 1769, talked his way through a few parties with him, wrote with enthusiasm about the manuscript, and never read it. D'Alembert said metaphysics was not his specialty. And Helvétius warned him to be cautious about publishing the system. M. de Voyer, Deschamps's sponsor, passed the manuscript off as his own, and for his pains got from Voltaire a grapeshot volley of skepticism about human nature and morals. Deschamps proved to be good litmus paper for testing the measure of the *philosophes'* commitments.

IV

The *philosophes* were more amenable to the *Nachlass* of the Curé Meslier, who had died many decades before, but only because they missed its eupsychian constructs. Being wafted up into a state of worldly eupsychia was clearly a professional hazard of members of the clergy who had lost their traditional faith. The *philosophes* welcomed in concert the anticlerical part of Meslier's doctrine. Only in the nineteenth and twentieth centuries were the rest of his writings published. There the social doctrines appear as an integral part of the attack on Christianity and are used to demonstrate that it could not be the true religion since it tolerated private property, inequality of status, and despotism.

Meslier was more violent than the monk of Saumur would ever

be. The powerful of the earth should be strangled with the guts of priests because both live in pleasure while the people suffer. Meslier's poststrangulation eupsychia is a world in which all men behave with justice and natural equity. In present society, on one side of the social barrier there reigns pride, on the other, hate. A few croak from overeating and the rest starve. One group live in a sort of paradise, the others languish in a hell. If all property were divided equally, everybody could be happy. If marriage were dissolvable, there would be no wretched conjugal unions. In the good future condition there will be a reasonable social hierarchy and a limited subordination; but men of the same parish will live in common, directed by the wisest and the best among them.

The Reverend William Godwin's anarchic commonalty was far less anti-intellectual than Deschamps's; but unlike the Benedictine's vision of a state of pure morality, Godwin's communal parishes could have recalcitrant members, and he resorts to psychic sanctions to bring them into line. Godwin delivered himself of grand excursions on the dynamic potentialities of absolute freedom. He pleaded for a wholesome state of mind, unloosed from shackles, in which every fiber of its frame is expanded according to the independent and individual impressions of truth upon it. But before his little anarchic parishes could function, there had to be a psychic revolution. The conviction had to become deeply engraved on the minds of all men that their genuine wants were their only just claim to the acquisition of goods. Unnecessarily consuming objects that might benefit another human being, or appropriating property to gain ascendancy over others, would in the future state become as abhorrent as committing murder. The psychological conversion had to precede the implementation of the utopia.

Not having heard of the tyranny of the big beast of public opinion in Stendhal's small town, Godwin proposed the little general will of parish neighbors as a preventive of crime in the future society. "No individual would be hardy enough in the cause of vice, to defy the general consent of sober judgment that would surround him. It would carry despair to his mind, or which is better, it would carry conviction. He would be obliged, by a force not less irresistible than whips and chains, to reform his conduct."[6] Something of the punitive spirit of Rousseau's *Social Contract* has seeped into the anarchic eupsychia of Godwin.

Alongside the ascetic communal eupsychians Deschamps, Meslier, and Godwin, who meant what they said and were all too ready for action programs, the Abbé Mably was only a salon communist. Mably associated private property with some sort of fall, either from Eden or the state of nature; and the acquisition of a sense of absolute property could be related to corruption and to an absence of Christian *caritas*. Private property was tainted and had to be redeemed in a new order of community. But for Mably such notions remained Platonic ideals; nothing would have horrified him more than to be classed with incendiary revolutionists, his fate after 1789. What he was declaiming against was the covetousness of the new men of enterprise, of large-scale industry and commerce, who cared nothing for community and a great deal about the free expression of their individuality in the marketplace. Mably's equality was something out of Plutarch's "Lycurgus" or out of Plato; it applied to no class and really meant no harm to anybody except the great bankers and entrepreneurs, who fell into the category of the conscienceless rich and could be castigated with impunity by the moralists.

Morelly, the unknown one, who may have been a schoolteacher, grounded his communal eupsychia on feelings of fraternity and humanity that would lead to the same natural ascetic egalitarianism. The first stage of Morelly's historical triad consisted of an original paternal government of one or more families characterized by sentiments of affection and tenderness among communal brethren in imitation of the fathers—remarkably unlike Freud's mythic primitive horde. The corruption of pristine communal feelings of sociability in the second stage of mankind came as a consequence of the multiplication of families and migrations. To inaugurate the third stage Morelly prescribed a reconstitution of agricultural communes and the imposition of tough sumptuary laws that would allow communal feelings to be revived. There would be rational work rules, strictly regulated conjugal relations, severe punishments for crime, all to reanimate the first natural law of sociability. For Morelley, more than the necessary would endanger equality, lead to the anti-eupsychian vice of luxuria, and destroy the fellow feeling which was the heart of his eupsychia.

Morelly is perhaps more important than the eupsychian clerics because his writing had a history. The *Code de la nature* enjoyed a certain notoriety in the eighteenth century since it was in print and was attributed to Diderot, while most of Meslier and all of Deschamps languished in manuscript. Godwin's volumes cost three guineas and were therefore declared innocuous by the British Government. But Morelly begat Babeuf and Babeuf drew from the *Code de la nature* the need for absolute equality, since the germs of envy and jealousy would grow if one man had more than another.

In the *Manifesto of the Equals*, that primary document of the modern communist utopia (probably composed by Babeuf's collaborator Sylvain Maréchal), Babeuf gave revolutionary content to Morelly's plan for agrarian communism, and stressed the equal need for food, which should be as free as sunshine and water. Equality for Babeuf required a continent, almost ascetic, community, in which shirkers would be severely punished. Equality became the ruling passion of the future ideal state of man. Complete, real equality, immediately established, was the paramount human need, not in its vague French Revolutionary sense, which could be twisted rhetorically in almost any economic or social direction, but in plain terms—one man should not have more of anything than another. If there is not enough to go round, you eliminate the thing itself, Babeuf insisted. This egalitarian communism is founded upon the idea of the virtual replication of needs, desires, and abilities among all citizens. Its intolerance of any distinctions is fierce. To be equal, not to suffer the pain of a superior's slights or power or authority—that was to set the tone of life, and all else was to be sacrificed to it. "We are equal, is it not so?" the *Manifesto* asked rhetorically, "Well, we henceforth intend to live and to die equal, just as we were born; we want real equality or death, that is what we *need*. And we shall have it, this *égalité réelle,* no matter what the price. . . . Woe to anyone who shall offer resistance to so keen a desire. . . . May all the arts be destroyed, as long as we have *égalité réelle*." [7] When Marx was confronted by the Babouvist ideal of instant and total equality he rejected it with contempt.

Another type of Enlightenment eupsychia is in sharp contradiction to the asceticism of the communal eupsychias. It concentrates on sexuality as the master of the soul. A basic opposition has to be established between those utopias that bestowed prime, if not exclusive, emphasis on a life of sensate stimulation as the source of pleasure, identifiable as happiness, and those that conceived of the ideal condition as the development of all human capacities beyond the instinctual. Kant's state of moral perfection to be achieved in history was the exemplar of this latter position, a philosophical stance that peremptorily rejected the worth of sensate happiness, while de Sade's utopias are the obvious culmination of the denial of *any* value in eupsychia other than immediate pleasurable stimulation of the multiple erotic zones either as an agent or as an object of sexual activity. A further polarity divided those sexual eupsychians that were committed to the immediacy of pleasurable fulfillment—again de Sade was the paradigmatic figure—from those that, like Restif, had a more intricate conceptualization of the delivery of maximal pleasure. Restif's eupsychias are dependent upon an elaborate system for placing impediments in the way of sexual fulfillment as a challenge and stimulus to desire, and upon a complex order of gratifications spread throughout the lifecycle to prevent boredom from overwhelming the pleasure seekers at any stage. De Sade's psychosexual ideal in one version is concentrated both on the immediacy and multiplication of sexual pleasures and on the sumptuary luxury that is to accompany supercharged gratification. Expansive sexuality becomes the primary reason for existence. Love and God and the laws are the great lies of civilization. The state is allowed to run its irrelevant business and is bought off with the idea that citizens gratified in all their parts will have neither the desire nor the energy to waste on the state and therefore it will be able to exercise easy control as long as it refrains from punishment. Present-day judicial punishments inflicted in cold blood are the Sadian anti-eupsychian crimes. Abolish virtually all laws and crime disappears, perhaps because there is no longer the perverse psychic need to commit crimes.

V

The eighteenth-century French Enlightenment reached a climax in the eupsychia of pure reason and dynamic science embodied in Condorcet's *Esquisse* and in his commentary on the *New Atlantis*. Condorcet has an interesting variation on the Rousseauan triadic stadial pattern. Once upon a time there were only natural inequalities. Then for some eight of the ten epochs of human history, *unnatural* inequalities held sway, as priests and tyrants seized power in a conspiracy of evil. Now and for all future time these unnatural inequalities will be virtually abolished as men move progressively toward a state of more or less equality, while warlike aggressive instincts become channeled into the exploitation of nature and, above all, science-making. In Condorcet's utopia of science man will be redeemed through the agency of the laws of social sciences—he used the term.

Despite the demarcation of ten stages in Condorcet's *Esquisse*, a sort of spilling over of the decimal system onto universal history, his sketch really falls into three distinct parts, he himself tells his readers in the introduction. The first is conjectural and is a progression that ends with alphabetical writing in Greece as the dividing mark; the second is an unbroken chain from alphabetical writing to the present, when men are close to one of the great revolutions of the human race; and the third is the infinite dynamic progress reserved for future generations. Unlike the German thinkers who make the last stage dependent upon the absorption of moral ideas into the psyche, Condorcet as *matérialiste* has to resort to the modification of man's biological nature through the transmission of acquired moral characteristics.

There is a dialectical quality to Condorcet's triad even though it is masked by a decimal front. In the very middle of the first tribal stage a counterforce to the history of reason is born—the formation of a class of men who are the repositories of the principles of knowledge, but who abuse their power by dividing the human race into two parts, those who control the instruments of knowledge and those who are forced to believe. The final eupsychian state will be one in which all men will have access to and participate in the increase of scientific knowledge, albeit in varying degrees, and the mathematical principles of a new social science will so dominate all conduct and legislation that the bifurcation of humanity into the learned and the ignorant will end. There would still be occasional intrusive passions, but they would be well under the control of mathematical reason. The ideal state of the soul is achieved when it becomes a science-making machine.

VI

Lest eupsychia appear to be an exclusive appanage of French Enlightenment thought in the eighteenth century, one must finally turn to the Germans. Among them no communal man raises his ugly head; nor is sexuality a permissible topic of psychic hope; and even science maintains a low profile. The German eupsychias are philosophical and abstract or aesthetic. Although their authors have left the community of orthodox believers, a theological odor lingers behind in their writings. As they hail the new man with somewhat varying degrees of enthusiasm, they too remain loyal to the triadic formula of Christian history.

Kant's whole history of the human species was a psychic drama in which the state of Antagonism—he used the English word—was the definition of radical evil, which would be overcome by the cunning of reason ushering in a state beyond animality, a condition that would witness the development of all human capacities beyond the instinctual. That is the eupsychia. Through multiple conflicts and trials and sufferings the human creature is likely to be forced to surrender *Habsucht, Ehrsucht,* and *Heerschsucht,* the three wicked drives for possession, status, and dominion, and to reach the state of moral beatitude. Of my gallery of eupsychians the Kant of his last essay, *Der Streit der Fakultäten* (1798), is perhaps the least confident.

Lessing's theological and Freemasonic formulations of the Third

Age represent the triumph of the truths of moral revelation internalized. Man will do the right because it is right, not because contingent rewards in the next world are annexed thereto, as in the Christian dispensation, the second stage of human education—rewards that formerly were intended simply to fix and strengthen his unsteady gaze. Perfected man will recognize the inner, finer rewards of well doing for its own sake. Lessing was conscious of the connection between his eupsychia, redolent of German Enlightenment theology, and the eternal Gospel of the Joachites. They both had had a glimpse of the three-stepped ascension to the new moral gospel; the fault of the Joachites lay only in their failure to allow for the maturation of the human race through time and for the penetration of the ethical teachings of the gospels into the inner man. The Joachites expected the moral truth of the reign of the Holy Ghost on earth to be revealed and internalized immediately. But Lessing understood that perfect illumination or loving virtue for its own sake could not be attained until the end of the eighteenth century.

Schiller employed another variant of the triadic metaphor in his critical review of the three stages of poetic expression in the Western world: The Greek was naïve, spontaneously reflecting nature; the intermediary stage was sentimental, disclosing a conflicted world in which the poet was at war with himself and with his surroundings; finally, the poet-teacher of a eupsychian age would reconcile the naïve quality of antiquity with the sentimental of modernity. By way of reason and freedom we return to nature, having traversed the stage of art and intellect. The historical rhythm still obeys the Christian-Rousseauan formula: original wholeness, conflicted duality, and at last an ideal unity.

After he has passed in review the varieties of eupsychian belief in the Enlightenment, what is a critical historian two centuries later to think of the achievements of the eupsychia-makers? Like most great stadial theorists they are powerful in evoking the fantasy of a past happiness, trenchant in their analysis of present ills, and imaginative or banal, according to taste, in drawing the portrait of future bliss. But all of their visions tend to fall apart at the intervals of transition. The hinges creak when one tries to open the doors leading from one stage to another. This is as true of the eighteenth-century eupsychias as it was of their far better known nineteenth-century successors. And yet as I reflect on how the eupsychian faithful of the eighteenth century have been faring in practice, it appears that, despite the prophets of doom, they have not done too badly. At least superficially, psychic egalitarianism and sexual emancipation have made their way in the Western world. As for the utopia of rationalist social science, though it appears to have had its triumphs, I am afraid we are confronting a body of illusory dogmas that will require a little army of Voltaires to combat. The internalized moral values of the German philosophico-aesthetic thinkers seem to have known the least progress. I must confess that I detect no such transformation as they foretold, either in myself or in my fellow men.

NOTES

CHAPTER 1

1. Jean Calvin, *Commentaries on the First Book of Moses, called Genesis,* trans. Rev. John King (Grand Rapids, Mich.: Eerdmans Publishing Co., 1948), vol. 1, pp. 85–87.

2. Lambert Daneau, *The Wonderfull Woorkmanship of the World,* trans. Thomas Twyne (London, 1578), p. 9.

3. Ibid., p. 10.

4. Johannes Kepler, *Nova Astronomia,* in *Gesammelte Werke,* ed. Walthar von Dyck and Max Caspar (Munich: Beck, 1937), vol. 3, p. 33.

5. Galileo Galilei, *Lettere copernicane* (Naples: Edizioni Glaux, n.d., [1959]), letter to the Grand Duchess Cristina, p. 98.

6. Kepler, *Nova Astronomia,* pp. 28–29.

7. Galileo, *Lettere copernicane,* letter to Cristina, p. 100.

8. Ibid.

9. *Johannes Kepler in seinem Briefen,* ed. Max Caspar and Walthar von Dyck (Munich and Berlin: R. Oldenbourg, 1930), vol. 1, p. 285, letter from Pistorius, Freiburg, July 12, 1607.

10. Ibid., vol. 2, p. 111.

11. Galileo, *Lettere copernicane,* letter to Cristina, p. 104.

12. Voltaire, *The Metaphysics of Sir Isaac Newton,* trans. David Erskine Baker (London, 1747), p. 3.

13. Richard Bentley, *Fourth Boyle Lecture,* June 6, 1692, in *Works,* ed. Alexander Dyce (London, 1838), vol. 3, p. 75.

14. Jerusalem, Jewish National and University Library, Yahuda MS. Var., Albert Einstein to A. S. Yahuda, September 1940, quoted in Frank E. Manuel, *The Religion of Isaac Newton* (Oxford: Clarendon Press, 1974), p. 27.

15. Yahuda MS. Var., A. S. Yahuda to Nathan Isaacs, 23 March 1941, quoting a conversation with George Sarton, cited in Manuel, *Religion of Isaac Newton,* p. 27.

16. William Whiston, *Sir Isaac Newton's Corollaries from his Philosophy and Chronology in his own Words* (London, 1729).

17. Yahuda MS. 15.5, fol. 98v, quoted in Manuel, *Religion of Isaac Newton*, p. 55.

18. Yahuda MS. 15.4, fol. 67v, quoted in Manuel, *Religion of Isaac Newton*, p. 61.

19. Yahuda MS. 15.5, fols. 96v, 97r, 98r, quoted in Manuel, *Religion of Isaac Newton*, p. 21.

20. Yahuda MS. 1.1, fol. 1r, quoted in Manuel, *Religion of Isaac Newton*, p. 88.

21. Ibid.

22. Yahuda MS 9.2, fol. 140 r, quoted in Manuel, *Religion of Isaac Newton*, pp. 101–102.

23. Yahuda MS. 1.1, fol. 14r, quoted in Manuel, *Religion of Isaac Newton*, pp. 48–49.

CHAPTER 2

1. Ralph Cudworth, *The True Intellectual System of the Universe* (London, 1678), p. 308.

2. John Toland, *Letters to Serena* (London, 1704), p. 71.

3. The 1720 edition was in Latin. Quotation is from the English translation, London, 1751, p. 5.

4. Toland, *Pantheisticon,* p. 56.

5. Ibid., p. 98.

6. *La Contagion sacrée, ou Histoire naturelle de la superstition. Ouvrage traduit de l'anglois* (London [Amsterdam], 1768) included a translation of *The Natural History of Superstition* in vol. 2, chaps. 12 and 13.

7. John Trenchard, *The Natural History of Superstition* (London, 1709), p. 9.

8. Nicolas Fréret, *Lettre de Thrasybule à Leucippe,* in *Oeuvres* (London, 1787), vol. 1, pp. 17–18.

9. Trenchard, *The Natural History of Superstition,* pp. 10–11.

10. Ibid., pp. 12–13.

11. Ibid., p. 13.

12. Ibid., p. 15.

13. Ibid., pp. 17–18.

14. Ibid., pp. 19–20.

15. Ibid., p. 28.

16. Anthony Ashley Cooper, Third Earl of Shaftesbury, *Characteristics of Men, Manners, Opinions, Times,* ed. John M. Robertson, with intro. by Stanley Grean (Indianapolis: Bobbs-Merrill, 1964), vol. 1, p. 192.

17. Ibid., p. 24.

18. Ibid., p. 12.

19. Ibid., p. 13.

20. *The Independent Whig,* December 31, 1720.

21. Trenchard, *The Natural History of Superstition,* p. 41.

22. Ibid., pp. 53–54.

CHAPTER 3

1. David Hume, *The Natural History of Religion,* ed. H. E. Root (Stanford, Calif.: Stanford University Press, 1957), p. 21.
2. Voltaire, *Dieu et les hommes* (1775), in *Oeuvres complètes,* vol. 33 (Paris, 1784), p. 238.
3. Diderot, *Essai sur la peinture pour faire suite au Salon de 1765,* in *Oeuvres complètes,* ed. J. Assézat and M. Tourneux, vol. 10 (Paris, 1876), p. 493.
4. Voltaire, *Dieu et les hommes,* p. 333.
5. Jerusalem, Jewish National and University Library, Yahuda MS 18.1, fol. 2v, quoted in Frank E. Manuel, *The Religion of Isaac Newton* (Oxford: Clarendon Press, 1974), p. 13.
6. Voltaire, *Dieu et les hommes,* pp. 177–78.
7. Paul Thiry, Baron d'Holbach, *La Contagion sacrée, ou Histoire naturelle de la superstition* (London [Amsterdam], 1768), pp. 111–12.
8. Rousseau, *Emile,* in *Oeuvres complètes* (Bibliothèque de la Pléiade), ed. Bernard Gagnebin and Marcel Raymond, vol. 4 (Paris: NRF, 1969), p. 607.

CHAPTER 4

1. Edward Gibbon, *Memoirs of My Life,* ed. Georges A. Bonnard (London: Nelson, 1966), pp. 103–4.
2. Gibbon, *Miscellaneous Works,* ed. John, Lord Sheffield (London, 1796), vol. 2, p. 717.
3. Gibbon, *Essai sur l'étude de la littérature* (London, 1761), p. 98.
4. *Essai,* p. 106.
5. *Essai,* p. 91.
6. Gibbon, *Letters,* ed. J. E. Norton (London: Cassell, 1956), vol. 1, p. 294, Gibbon to Holroyd, October 1, 1771.
7. *Essai,* p. 108.
8. *Essai,* p. 109.
9. Paul Robert, *Dictionnaire alphabétique et analogique de la langue française* (Paris: Société du nouveau Littré, 1966), vol. 5, p. 859.
10. Gibbon, *The History of the Decline and Fall of the Roman Empire,* vol. 6 (London, 1788), p. 645 (chap. 71).
11. *Essai,* p. 92.
12. *Essai,* p. 85.
13. New York, John Pierpont Morgan Library, *Catalogue de la bibliothèque de M. Gibbon; fait à Lausanne le 16 septembre, 1785* (manuscript, not in Gibbon's hand).
14. In the *History,* vol. 2 (1781), p. 61, Gibbon mockingly controverts Montesquieu's establishment of the relationship between freedom and low taxes as "an invariable law of nature."
15. Gibbon, *Miscellaneous Works,* vol. 2, p. 619.
16. *Letters,* vol. 3, p. 317, Gibbon to Lord Sheffield, February 9–18, 1793.

17. General John Meredith Read, Jr., *Historic Studies in Vaud, Berne, and Savoy* (London, 1897), vol. 2, p. 297.

18. Geoffrey Keynes, *The Library of Edward Gibbon* (London, 1940).

19. *History*, vol. 6, p. 629.

20. *Letters*, vol. 2, p. 122, Gibbon to J. B. Suard, November 8, 1776.

21. *Miscellaneous Works*, vol. 2, p. 639.

22. Gibbon read Mably's *Parallèle des Français et des Romains* on November 4, 1763; *Miscellaneous Works*, vol. 2, p. 219.

23. *Letters*, vol. 2, p. 127, Gibbon to Suzanne Necker, November 26, 1776.

24. Ibid., p. 218, Gibbon to Georges Deyverdun, June 4, 1779. Gibbon is probably referring to Horace's mutum et turpe pecus.

25. Ibid., p. 169, Gibbon to Dorothea Gibbon, December 16, 1777.

26. Ibid., p. 326, Gibbon to Georges Deyverdun, May 20, 1783.

27. Condorcet, *Esquisse d'un tableau historique des progrès de l'esprit humain*, 4th ed. (Genoa, 1798), p. 313.

28. *History*, vol. 3 (1781), "General Observations" (following chap. 38), p. 635.

29. Ibid., p. 636.

30. Keynes, *The Library of Gibbon*.

31. *History*, vol. 3, pp. 639–40.

32. Turgot, *Oeuvres*, ed. Gustave Schelle (Paris, 1913), vol. 1, p. 133.

33. *History*, vol. 5 (1788), chap. 53, p. 517.

34. Ibid., p. 515.

35. A letter of October 9, 1793, to Lord Sheffield reads: "The troubles of Bristol have been serious and bloody: I know not who was in fault, but I do not like the appeasing the mob. . . ."; *Letters*, vol. 3, p. 353.

36. Ibid., p. 171, Gibbon to Lord Sheffield, September 25, 1789.

37. Ibid., p. 184, Gibbon to Lord Sheffield, December 15, 1789.

38. Ibid., p. 321, Gibbon to Lord Loughborough, February 23, 1793.

39. Ibid., p. 318, Gibbon to Lord Sheffield, February 18, 1793.

40. *History*, vol. 3, p. 631, "General Observations on the Fall of the Roman Empire in the West."

CHAPTER 5

1. Humphrey Prideaux, *The Old and New Testament Connected in the History of the Jews and Neighboring Nations from the Declension of the Kingdoms of Israel and Judah to the Time of Christ*, 2 vols. (London, 1716–18).

2. The second book of Harrington's *The Art of Law-giving* (London, 1659) is described as "shewing the frames of the Commonwealth of Israel and of the Jewes."

3. Judah Monis, *The truth, being a discourse which the author delivered at his baptism. Containing nine principal arguments the modern Jewish rabbins do make to prove the Messiah is yet to come; with the answer to each . . . and likewise with the confession of his faith*. Pref-ac'd by the Rev. Increase Mather (Boston, 1722).

4. John Lightfoot, *Horae Hebraicae et Talmudicae in quatuor Evangelistas cum tractatibus chorographicis, singulis suo Evangelistae praemissis* (Leipzig, 1684).

5. Dom Augustin Calmet, *Commentaire littéral sur tous les livres de l'Ancien et du Nouveau Testament,* 23 tomes in 22 vols. (Paris, 1707–16).

6. Leningrad. Publichnaia biblioteka, *Biblioteka Vol'tera. Katalog Knig* (Moscow, 1961), p. 628, no. 2469.

7. Voltaire, *Correspondence,* ed. Theodore Besterman, vol. 93 (Geneva: Institut et Musée Voltaire, 1964), p. 140, no. 18819, Voltaire to Nicolas Toussaint Le Moyne dit Des Essarts, February 26, 1776.

8. Antoine Guenée, *Lettres de quelques juifs portugais allemands et polonais à M. de Voltaire* (Paris, 1769).

9. Voltaire, *Complete Works,* ed. Theodore Besterman, "Key to Pseudonyms and Nicknames," in vol. 135 (Oxford: The Voltaire Foundation at the Taylor Institution, 1977), p. 985.

10. Gotthold Ephraim Lessing, *Die Erziehung des Menschengeschlechts* (1780).

11. Voltaire, *Correspondence,* vol. 58 (1960), p. 8, no. 11672, Voltaire to Charles Augustin Feriol, Comte d'Argental, and Jeanne Grâce Bosc Du Bouchet, Comtesse d'Argental, April 3, 1765.

12. Ibid., vol. 52 (1960), p. 127, no. 10440, Voltaire to the Comte and Comtesse d'Argental, June 10, 1763.

13. Ibid., vol. 49 (1959), p. 131, no. 9791, Voltaire to Isaac de Pinto, July 21, 1762.

14. *Israel vengé, ou Exposition naturelle des prophéties hébraiques que les chrétiens appliquent à Jésus, leur prétendu messie* (London, 1770). Orobio's work was entitled: *Prevenciones divinas contra la vana idolatria de las Gentes.*

15. John Spencer, *De legibus Hebraeorum ritualibus et eorum rationibus, libri tres* (Cambridge, 1683–85).

16. David Hume, *The Natural History of Religion* (1757), ed. H. E. Root (Stanford, Calif.: Stanford University Press, 1957), pp. 46–48.

17. See Jefferson's copy of Holbach's *Le Bon-sens ou Idées naturelles opposées aux idées surnaturelles* (London [Amsterdam], 1772), with manuscript notes on the front flyleaf and in the margins (Houghton Library, Harvard University).

18. Paul Henri Thiry, Baron d'Holbach, *L'Esprit du Judaïsme, ou Examen raisonné de la loi de Moyse, & de son influence sur la religion chrétienne* (London, 1770), pp. 175–76.

19. Ibid., pp. 171–73.

20. Ibid., p. 169.

21. J. G. Herder, *Vom Geist der ebräischen Poesie* (1782).

22. Moses Mendelssohn, *Gesammelte Schriften,* ed. G. B. Mendelssohn (Leipzig, 1844), vol. 5, p. 505, Moses Mendelssohn to Hofrath Michaelis in Göttingen, ca. Nov. 1770: "I feel certain that you will treat the Psalms as poetry, without regard to the prophetic and the mystical which Christian as well as Jewish expositors found in the Psalms only because they looked for them there; and they only looked for them because they were

neither philosophers nor judges of literature." On the relations of Mendelssohn and Johann David Michaelis, see Alexander Altmann, *Moses Mendelssohn. A Biographical Study* (Philadelphia: Jewish Publication Society of America, 1973), pp. 242–44, where this letter is paraphrased. I owe the reference to Professor Altman.

23. Mendelssohn, *Jerusalem, oder über religiöse Macht und Judentum* (Berlin, 1783).

24. Edward Gibbon, *Decline and Fall of the Roman Empire,* chap. 2, section 1.

25. *Commentary on the Documents of Vatican II* (New York: Herder, 1969), vol. 3, pp. 67–71.

26. *The Sixteen Documents of Vatican II and the Instruction on the Liturgy* (Boston: Daughters of St. Paul, 1966), pp. 255–60. The official title of the document is: "Declaratio de Ecclesiae habitudine ad religiones non-Christianas."

CHAPTER 6

1. Johann Gottfried Herder, *Sämmtliche Werke,* ed. Bernard Suphan (Berlin, 1877–1913).

2. Rudolf Haym, *Herder nach seinem Leben und seinen Werken* (Berlin, 1880, 1885).

3. *Outlines of a Philosophy of the History of Man,* trans. T. O. Churchill (London, 1800), vol. 1, p. vii.

4. Ibid., p. viii.

5. Ibid.

6. Ibid.

7. *Briefe zu Beförderung der Humanität,* in *Sämmtliche Werke,* ed. Suphan, vol. 3, p. 8.

8. *Philosophy of History,* trans. Churchill, vol. 1, p. 166.

9. Ibid.

10. *Ideen zur Philosophie der Geschichte der Menschheit,* in *Sämmtliche Werke,* ed. Suphan, vol. 13, p. 276. See also Churchill translation, vol. 2, pp. 157–59.

11. *Philosophy of History,* trans. Churchill, vol. 1, p. 305.

12. Ibid., p. 149.

13. *Ideen zur Philosophie der Geschichte der Menschheit,* in *Sämmtliche Werke,* ed. Suphan, vol. 13, p. 287.

14. Ibid.

15. *Philosophy of History,* trans. Churchill, vol. 2, p. 175.

16. *Aelteste Urkunde des Menschengeschlects* (1774), in *Sämmtliche Werke,* ed. Suphan, vol. 6, p. 215.

17. Ibid., p. 387.

18. *Sämmtliche Werke,* ed. Suphan, vol. 6, p. 113.

19. *Aelteste Urkunde,* in *Sämmtliche Werke,* ed. Suphan, vol. 6, p. 370.

CHAPTER 7

1. Eupsychia is a neologism invented by my friend the late Professor Abraham H. Maslow. I trust he will pardon my transformation of the term into a historical category of limited generality.

2. *Le Vrai système* remained in manuscript until it was edited and published by Jean Thomas and Franco Venturi (Geneva: Droz, 1963).

3. Jean Meslier, *Oeuvres complètes,* ed. Jean Deprun et al., 3 vols. (Paris: Editions Anthropos, 1970–72).

4. Written in 1785, the work was first published by Eugen Dühren in Berlin, 1904.

5. *Zum ewigen Frieden: Ein philosophischer Entwurf* first appeared in Königsberg, 1795.

6. William Godwin, *Political Justice* (London, 1793), vol. 2, p. 116.

7. Filippo Michele Buonarroti, *Conspiration pour l'égalité dite de Babeuf* (1828), new ed. (Paris: Editions sociales, 1957), vol. 2, pp. 94–95.

INDEX